Manage **Your** Money, Manage **Your** Self, Achieve **Your** goals

By S L Clay

I0474980

First published in 2011
Copyright ©2011 by Scott L Clay.
The moral rights of the author has been asserted.

Contents

Introduction

This book has been written to be a simple and straightforward guide for people just like you who want some practical ideas on how to help achieve your goals. Many books are written on this subject which I do not feel give people any handle on what they should actually be doing, and how to actually go about making real changes to what they currently do on a day to day basis. Too many books are written by people offering high level, woolly ideas without any real substance or obvious method to apply what they suggest.

To get where you want to go I feel you need to address two key areas, your financial position and how you interact and go about your business on a day to day basis.

So how will controlling your money, help you control your life? Well 8 out of 10 people with money concerns say their money worries have a negative effect on other areas of their lives, impacting on their work and career as well as personal relationships and health. It therefore stands to reason that to get your life and ambitions moving, then you need to address your financial concerns first. All too many books are published giving all manner of advice on how to boost your career, gain promotions, start your own business, offering advice on motivation, but all too many people read the advice given, but do not act on it, why?

Well for a number of reasons, but the most common is due to their financial situation, debt, lack of income, financial commitments or quite simply they just don't know how to organise and control their money in a manner that will get them moving in the right direction. The most common reasons I hear for people not starting their own business, taking a course and re-training, making a change in career or just not taking the next step in life is they don't have the money or the time.

There are a large number of books offering help with your money, which is fine. However many of them give advice on how to save money, spend less, prepare endless monthly budgets and in a rather nagging and condescending fashion, to be more prudent with your money. They don't give us a new perspective on money or a basic grounding in what financial products are out there and how they work. The reality is people read these books with all the best intentions, much in same way they make new-year resolutions to join the gym and start a diet. Ask yourself, what happens? They go to the gym very regularly for the first few weeks, then it drops to twice a week, then once per month, you get the picture. By summer time they can't remember where the gym membership card is and as for diets, that half eaten pack of rice bread spends the rest of the year in the back of the cupboard.

The interesting thing about people who write books on finance and money is that they are usually coming at it from personal experience, great for them but not necessarily for the person reading the book? Just because they are now successful, what worked for them previously, may not necessarily work for you now. Their success may have been twenty years ago which means the methods and ways which worked then, may not work now. Furthermore rarely do they have any qualifications to give financial advice, so based on this, what qualifies them to give advice on money matters?

As I write this now, I am a qualified financial adviser, regulated and authorised by the Financial Services Authority (FSA). I started my own financial services firm at the start of the credit crunch (good timing, I know!) We deal with clients on a daily basis with all manner of different financial circumstances. I have worked for wealthy clients and clients on low incomes

6

struggling to make ends meet. Regardless of the client however, they always have issues to address. I have also helped people who have been in serious financial difficulties. I think this makes me more qualified than most authors to provide practical advice on money matters, because I have seen and helped many clients with a wide range of financial issues. I have also worked for a major UK bank and have spoken with all manner of customers and have seen spending patterns from a wide range of different customers. I have viewed bank accounts belonging to people with gambling problems, shopaholics, pensioners who hoard vast sums in zero interest accounts, I have seen almost every imaginable set of account details and you would be shocked to see how some people manage their money.

But what has really driven me to write this book, is that all other books seem to miss the point, in that our money and our lives are intrinsically linked. You can write a motivational or self improvement book which really inspires others, it may make people think differently about their lives and truly motivate them to change their life for the better. But because you have debts, have a large mortgage repayment, money to repay on credit cards as well as a family to look after, that motivation can quickly fade. What use is motivation alone without a credible plan to move you forward?
You work in a 9 – 5 job where you are tied to a desk and are working hard to keep the job, as well as trying to find some time for a social life. Your income and outgoings are almost the same amount each month. So when are you suppose to have time to do the things you really want to do, start that business, apply for the new job, create a property empire?

For many of us, it is difficult because of financial commitments, it is difficult to break the chain and make the break. Or should I say, make the break but de-risk the situation.

What this book is about is real-world, practical, applicable ideas to address your overall situation and allow you to start achieving your goals. Crucially it addresses issues concerning your money and finances with practical plans to get you where you need to be financially. I did it and so can you, but it is not always easy and does require lots of work and commitment.

Importantly you will see many references to self-discipline and I encourage you to make this a good habit to get into as quickly as possible. Therefore start now and take control and management of your own expectations. This book alone will not guarantee you will achieve your goals, however what it will do is give you the fuel for the tank, but you have to drive the journey.

What I suggest you do is to make a start today. The journey of a thousand miles starts with one step, and you want to make it today. So start today. Read a little more and you will already have some good ideas on how to get started. If you are worried about a debt on a credit card, start this month and repay a little more off. Remember the course you wanted to apply for but never did? Make a start this evening and fill out the application form. You will be amazed how better you feel just by taking the very first small steps in the right direction. Why not spend an hour tidying up your paperwork and filing those bank statements in order – trust me it all works.
What comes next is the discipline and commitment to see it through, anyone can start something, and it is only the truly strong of mind that see things through to the end. How many people do you know have started things and subsequently quit or dropped out? Don't be one of them, be strong and stick the course. Start reading this book and make sure you get to the end. If you decide to make changes to your life, do it and stick to it. Do not wimp out.

So prepare the world to look out for you, your coming, you are making the start now and your progress will be swift, you are just as capable as anyone else out there so why shouldn't you realise your goals and aspirations? Have a look at some of the heads of industry and business leaders, very rarely will you see a scientist or someone with a PHD running a major corporation earning a six or seven figure salary. It's the workers, the grafters, the people who get up early and work late, the ones who don't take no for an answer and the ones with the drive.

Last time I checked, all those qualities are free of charge. Furthermore there is nothing stopping you from adopting them tomorrow, is there? So start tomorrow, get up earlier, get into work early and start working towards your goals.

I hope you enjoy the book, take on board the ideas, you don't have to agree with them all, take the ones that work for you, make them your own and get them working for you, and Good luck!

It is infinitely better to plunge ahead and do what is required, than it is to question your abilities and be paralysed by doubt.
(Unknown)

Genius is one percent inspiration and ninety-nine percent perspiration
(Edison, 1847 - 1931)

Manage Your Finances

Understanding Money & Wealth

Many people don't understand money, they just don't get it. Despite working all their lives for it, looking forward to pay-day to get it, usually carrying it with them where ever they go and often spending more than they have, people rarely have a real understanding of money and how to use it and manipulate it for their own good.

We try to save some of it, many of us really like spending it and actually a lot of us allow it to dictate and restrict what you can do, and sometimes, letting it cause us stress and breakdown of families.

We often hear the phrase that some people are just not good with money, but that is nonsense, it is not part of their DNA to just be bad with money, it is much simpler than that. Someone who is bad with money typically refers to someone who spends most of their money and doesn't plan what to do with it. That's usually the case.

Therefore it stands to reason that anyone can be good with money, all you need is a plan, then stick to it. You will instantly see an improvement in your circumstances. This book is full of ideas you can use to make you, good with money.

One simple thing I started many years ago was collecting money. I have 5 jars in my office. The quality street jar contains coppers, so does the large glass one, the whiskey bottle is almost full with 5p's, the coffee glass contains silver and the other glass contains Euros. What I do after every day is take out the change from my pockets and add it to the correct jar. It is great because every day I see the jars slowly filling up, saving more and more.

I think of it as a collection in the exact same way someone collects stamps, comic books or Toby jugs, I collect coins, not ancient or old coins, but every day coins in my jars.
I am very reluctant to ever dip into my jars, because then my collection goes down, in the same way the comic book collector would never sell their rarest comics, I don't spend my coins.

Now this is a very simple method to make you better with money, it might work for you, but don't worry if it doesn't, either way it is just one thing that may help and is an example of how simple ideas can make a change to your habits for the better. What you need to do is find out what works for you, then crucially, stick to it and make it a habit.

Ever heard people talk about rich people being tight with their money? Ever heard someone say "he is only rich because he never spends anything"?
Well surely that's correct? If you spend money you have less, and if you don't spend you have more. One thing our modern day culture portrays is that spending money is a sign of wealth, well maybe but for how long? Once you have spent all your money, you are not rich any more, that's for certain!
So my advice is this, consider money as a precious resource, much like you would on a desert island with water. Look after it, treat it as something precious, not to be wasted and easily parted with. Think of it as something you want to keep and hold onto.

If you want to feel rich, just count the things you have that money cannot buy
(Unknown)

A fool and his money are soon parted
(Tusser)

Don't budget monthly – do it once & make a plan

Don't make a monthly budget. It is a complete waste of time. Your financial position changes on a daily basis, how can you be expected to make a budget of your monthly outgoings if it is constantly changing? Is your phone bill identical every month, or does it depend on the number of calls you make? Is it the same price each month for water, gas and electricity? I don't know anyone who rushes home to update a spreadsheet of their personal monthly budget every time they spend money or receive a bill in the post? Many books preach this but I feel it is nonsensical – why plan to do something if you know you are not going to do it? Do not set yourself unrealistic objectives.

The best way to manage your money on a monthly basis is simple - make a budget once, then make a plan, and then stick to it. Check it every 3 – 6 months. Keeping a plan simple and straightforward ensures you are more likely to stick to it. Creating a complicated spreadsheet with all manner of formulas and expecting yourself to update it by the hour, is never going to work or last.

To make your budget, I suggest trying the following:
Make a list of your category 1 commitments. These are the crucial commitments which must be paid, mortgage, loan repayment, council tax and utility bills. Remember post-credit crunch your credit rating is becoming ever more important in the eyes of lenders, so don't let a poor credit rating get in the way of your plans, do not miss nor be late with any of the Category 1 payments.

Category 2 are payments of less importance but still have to be paid as it's a commitment you have agreed to or most likely plays a significant role in your day-to-day life. These include phone bills, petrol and travel costs – you have to get to work somehow.

The Category 3 payments are ones which you have opted to pay but could probably cancel if needed. These payments tend to be the luxuries in life, which may not be necessities but the little indulgencies that make everything worthwhile. Now this book is not about how to save money – but reviewing and possibly cancelling some of these payments could save you money.

For example using the table below, cancelling all Category 3 commitments, you would instantly save £280 per month using the example below. There you go, you have just created the additional money needed to start you on your quest to achieve your goals. Now you could argue the golf membership may enhance your chances of networking and meeting the right people, however multi channel TV? – get rid of it now, you don't watch all those channels, I know you don't! If you want to save money, Category 3 will most likely contain the ones which you could strip from your budget and save money. That said, it probably contains some nice luxuries which you may be reluctant to give up. So be disciplined, think about the bigger picture, do you really watch all 3,000 channels, is achieving your goals more important than Celebrity Talent Jungle Factor On-ice?

Category 1		Category 2		Category 3	
Mortgage	£600	Phone Line	£25	Gym	£45
Council Tax	£94	Mobile	£35	Sky / Cable	£55
Gas/Elec	£49	Internet	£20	Season Ticket	£60
Loan	£120	Petrol	£100	Golf Membership	£120
Credit Card	£60	Rail	£15		
Car Payment	£120				
Insurances	£120				
TOTALS	**£1,163**		**£195**		**£280**

All figures per month

When it comes to budgeting I would strongly recommend paying as many bills as you can on direct debt.
Some reasons why:

- You can get a list of all your DD's from the bank, makes it easier to see all outgoings on one sheet when budgeting
- Helps to ensure you don't miss a payment or have a late payment on your credit file
- You retain control and can still cancel them if needed
- Bills are still paid when you are on holiday etc

I also recommend joining one of the credit reference agencies, Experian or Equifax to track your credit profile. I cannot stress how important this information will be in the future. If you need to borrow money, short or long term, then this will be vital. Keep track of it and don't bury your head in the sand, if there are any issues address them head on. No one is perfect when it comes to managing money, but it shouldn't stop you from trying to be. Be open and honest about your financial position with yourself and with others.

I once did a budget and at the time, my income essentially matched my outgoings and left me with almost zero disposable income, literally about £5. As such, I got a second job, I cancelled a lot of my Cat 3 commitments, reviewed all current bills for better deals and paid down debt and got myself in to a much better position within just six months. If I had buried my head in the sand and ignored the situation it could have been much worse.

Some couples go over their budgets very carefully. Others just go over them

(Mansfield, 1888 - 1923)

Make saving a commitment just like the bills

Every month you should try and save some money. Not as much as you can, but something and any reasonable amount will do. By that, I mean an amount you can do without. Not an amount which is too much one month and then requires you to withdraw the same amount next month from your savings because you are short of cash!

Depending on where you are in your life will determine how much you can afford to put away, but try and put something away no matter how small.

The second thing is to then leave it and don't touch it again – think of it as money that you have spent and as such will not get back, that way you don't miss it and you will be reluctant to withdraw on it.

I have seen so many people set up an ISA with great intentions at the start of the tax year and pay money in straight away. Great! But then the following month they withdraw some money from it, the next month its empty and it stays empty till the end of the year.

Remember the budget we did earlier? Guess what you should add to your Category 1 commitments? Yes, savings, no matter how small, make saving a Category 1 commitment and as such it's something which needs to be paid in the exact same way that you must pay the mortgage. If you do this, it will automatically be taken care of and your spends still remains your spends. You should aim to make saving a commitment that you stick to. Remember - discipline!

Once you have started don't stop and stick at it, don't even check the balance on the savings account either, just let it sit there and grow. You have other things to focus on like your career and achieving your goals so don't be tempted to treat yourself to a holiday with the money you save. We are building long term wealth not short term savings for Magaluf!

Now this book is not strictly focused on pure financial advice and for that I suggest you speak with a financial adviser. The later chapters look at saving and investing in more detail, however the basics you should consider are as follows.

You should always aim to keep a couple of month's salary in an instant access savings account. This money can cover short term emergencies or anything unexpected. If we are saving for a period of 5 years or less then you should think about NS&I premium bonds and savings or possibly a bank savings account. You should also aim to shelter these savings from the Tax man so I suggest considering a cash ISA whenever possible. The ISA is essentially a wrapper placed around the savings account and ensures the tax man knows not to tax you on any gains within the ISA. Remember rates from Banks are awfully low, so shop around or speak with an IFA.
For savings of five years or more, you should consider investing. This again can be within an ISA but investments have the potential for greater gains over the long term. It is not guaranteed like a savings account, but over the long term, history shows us, that on average you will get a better return by investing.

Much of how you save is down to you and your personal preference and most crucial of all, it's about what you are saving for. If you are saving money so you can quit your job and start your own business, you may take a different approach than if you are saving for retirement or your Childs university fees.
Regardless, it is your money and you want to get it working hard for you, not for a faceless and morally corrupt banking corporation.

The pain of discipline is a lot less severe, than the pain of failure
(Bombell)

Don't count every penny, just work out your spends

Once you have done your budget once, stick to it, all that is left is to work out what you have left. This money is then yours, it's your disposable income (I don't like that phrase, money should never be something to be 'disposed' of) but it's your cash to do with as you please.

This is an important junction in your decision making process. Do you blow this money on good times, self indulgence, parties, expensive clothes and nights out, or, do you use this money to start building your empire and start putting it into something which will help you achieve your goals? Do you get this money working for you?

Either way, making a budget for every penny is unpractical for most people, myself included. I simply total all my outgoings, deduct this from my income and that is my disposable money. This is much easier to do, it takes a lot less time and because of this I am more likely to actually do it each month!

Another tip is have two bank accounts, one for the bills and one into which you receive your income. This is what I have done for a number of years and it really helps to manage my money.
One account receives all the income, salary and other income I receive. I then make one transfer to another account which is my bills account. I transfer a substantial sum across and this ensures all the direct debts on the bills account are paid. The sum remaining in my account is my money. I don't have an overdraft on this account either ensuring I can only spend what I earn and no more.

If your struggling for discipline with this one, simply withdraw your spends from the bank as cash and put it in your wallet. Once it's gone, it's gone. Ok, so if you lose your wallet it will be gone even faster so don't lose it! However studies show that people spend less when its actual cash in their pocket, for some reason, psychologically, we don't seem to think of spending money when it's done on a plastic card.

As mentioned above, your spends doesn't have to be spent. Of your disposable income, how much of this are you going to save? I mentioned in the previous chapter that savings should be added to your Cat1 commitments so let's assume you have decided already to save X amount per month. The remaining money is yours – so what will you do with it? You must have little treats each month, the odd meal out, DVD box set, tickets to a game. But do not over-do it and of your spends I would also try and save most of that as well.

The point is this – are you fixed on achieving your goals, do you really have a burning desire inside you to get ahead or do you have a more casual approach? Yes, you would like to be rich and own that villa in Spain, but it does it matter to you if it never happens? It is exactly this approach which can determine the final outcome.

It is your money and you want to get it working for you.

Money is not the most important thing in the world, love is. Fortunately I love money
(Mason)

Saving and Investing

I mentioned earlier that your commitment to savings should be just as important as your mortgage payment. Therefore let's assume you agree and have decided to save £250 per month, every month from now onwards. What can you do with this money?

There are a wide range of savings and investment vehicles out there offering a wide range of options. This book is not a guide to investments or finance, however the following chapters give a high level overview of the potential options that are available, into which you can invest your money.

You could put it in a savings account with the bank. You could open an ISA and invest in some funds. You could pay it into a pension (but you cannot touch it again till you are 55, so not good for short term saving) which could be a wise move. The reality is that it all depends on what you are saving for and what your goal is.

What I can say regarding saving and investing is that it made Warren Buffet the richest man on the earth at one point – he is now slumming it in 3rd place with only $50billion. He started investing in companies from an early age, he invested so much in some companies that he ended up owning the majority of the company.
The reality of investing is that it can be considered high risk, and you could actually get back less than you put in, but that is all relative.

If you invest £100 in BP shares today and the share price falls by 50% tomorrow, at which point you decided to sell your shares, then yes you would lose money and you would also be an idiot, all at the same time. If the stock price does go down by 50%, rather than sell, you decided to hold on to the shares over the long term, than history shows us that you are likely to get a positive return assuming there are no fundamental problems with the company, plus you would also get dividend payments as well. That is assuming the company in question returned to its normal business over the long term.

Like many things in life, it is all relative and depends on your attitude to investing and what your plans and goals are. The only real way you can 'lose it all' investing in shares is if you invest money in high risk start-up businesses that subsequently goes bust with debt, there is a chance then you would lose it all. So it is simply really, don't invest in high risk shares and you will not lose it all!

As for saving in an ISA or deposit account, this can be a wise move, you just need to check on the rate you will get. See the section on inflation to understand why you need a good rate on your savings.

Finally all savings should be as tax efficient as possible. You should always try and use your ISA allowance every year before investing in anything else and you should also try and use up your other tax free allowances assuming you are entitled to them. Again speak with an Independent Financial Adviser who can advise on the best way to do this.

A public opinion poll, is no substitute for thought

I don't jump over 7ft bars, I look for 1ft bars which I can step over

If past history is all there is to investing, then librarians would be the richest amongst us

In the 20th century, the United States endured two world wars and other traumatic and expensive military conflicts; the Depression; a dozen or so recessions and financial panics; oil shocks; a flu epidemic; and the resignation of a disgraced president. Yet the Dow rose from 66 to 11,497

(Buffet)

Property

Property is an interesting concept in terms of investment as it also plays the vital role, in literally, providing a roof above our heads. The majority of us purchase a property (often via a mortgage) to be our home in which we plan to live and reside. However what we saw in the UK between 2003 and 2007 was a dramatic rise in property prices coupled with a liberal attitude by lenders to offer mortgages at very competitive rates. What resulted was a speculative attitude amongst many people in the UK who started to view property as a rock solid investment, one which could replace the need even for a pension. People realised their own property had increased significantly in value, some people took additional loans against their home to allow them to purchase additional property with the plan to rent the property and receive an income and capital growth. And so the market continued and the bubble was created - which eventually burst.

That covers a specific amount of time, however historically UK property has shown time and again over the long term to represent a good investment in terms of capital growth and has often outpaced inflation. It is also rather easy to get into the market, because as soon as you have purchased your first property, then you're already in the market or more often referred to as 'on the property ladder'.
What some people do is live in their property for a number of years, as the property grows in value they use this opportunity to trade up and move into a bigger property, often to accommodate a growing family. Some people can choose to stay in the property and re-mortgage to extract the equity into cash to lavish on cars, holidays or home improvements.
Some people purchase a property to subsequently sell on a few months later, during which time they plan to carry out improvements either structurally or cosmetically, which they feel will add value to the property and increase the selling price resulting in a profit.

Finally some people choose to purchase properties purely to rent them out as part of a property portfolio. Some professional landlords can own a large number of properties and run them as a business, the rental income providing the bulk of the income for the business, with maintenance and mortgage repayments/finance costs often being the biggest outgoings.

As you can see there are a range of options when it comes to property. But it is just one asset class and as such if you have all your wealth tied up in property, then all you need is a housing market crash to massively reduce the value of your assets. Furthermore, a slump in the rental market and a dip in demand, can severely affect your income and ability to service mortgages or other debts on your properties. Finally property is not liquid and it can take months to liquefy your assets and release some cash, in a falling market this can compound this issue. Therefore most financial advisers would advise on a balanced portfolio of wealth with property being just one of many asset classes. A ten year slump in the property market means a lost decade for your money, it would be pointless to sell properties when the market crashes as you will get the lowest price, it is worth holding on and not selling. During which time markets in Asia could be booming and experiencing 10% growth, you could be investing there - but you cannot as your cash is all tied up in property and will be for another few years. That is a very gloomy picture but it could easily be a reality. It will be interesting to see where the UK property market goes in the next 5 years, my guess is it will be flat and remain so for some years to come whilst the rest of the problems in the economy iron themselves out.

Buy land, they are not making it anymore

(Twain)

Cash & Savings

Cash and Savings are money in the bank, rock solid, sound and secure? Well don't be too quick to assume that, but on the whole, yes you are right. However before 2008, you wouldn't have believed that any bank in the UK could go bust – well we saw that all too well recently, so don't forget some banks can fail and take your money with them. That said, in the UK, the government insures the first part of your savings, up to the value of approx £85,000 which brings the UK into line with the rest of Europe. That is per financial institution so if you are the sort who likes to keep lots of cash in the bank, keep up to £85,000 in one bank and the rest in another. By doing this you are guaranteeing all your money. So basically, if the bank goes bust, the government step in and guarantee your money.

The problem with cash in the bank is that it doesn't tend to grow much, at least not in real terms. The bank may pay you (based on current rates) between 1-3% interest on your money which sounds ok as you are getting interest on the money you have in the bank. However if inflation is between 1-3% then in fact your getting nothing. Your money is not growing, you are not getting wealthier and you're getting zero return on your money – all in real terms.

However money in the bank again is a form of asset class and you should aim to have a pot of cash in the bank before you decided to invest in property or stocks or any other asset classes. Cash in the bank should be your emergency reserve to cover any short term expenses or emergency such as a new boiler etc. Long term, you should try and avoid keeping the bulk of your wealth in cash, history shows us that your wealth will be outpaced by shares and property over the long term. There is no point in building a sand castle to sit by and watch the sea erode it away over time.

However in all humans we have an inbuilt safety meter which may have been programmed by parents or grandparents, or may be highly influenced by some negative previous experience you may have had with money. Either way this is often our default safety setting which says keep cash in the bank. My advice is don't fight it, if it keeps you happy then do it. Just remember you will have to keep paying more into savings as your money will not be working as hard for you as it could be.

Whoever said money cannot buy happiness simply didn't know where to go shopping

(Derek)

The art is not in making money, but in keeping it

(Unknown)

Shares, Funds, Bonds & Financial Investments

This asset class is often viewed as very complex and technical, simply the mention of stocks and shares tends to bemuse and deter most people. The reality is actually very simple and thanks to the internet, investing in shares has never been easier.

Shares are actually very simple to understand. Imagine you have some money but are unsure what to do with it. Your friend however tells you they have started their own computer company which is going really well, making lots of profit and he is very keen to expand the business.
You think to yourself that you would like to be part of this, but you have no computer knowledge and therefore cannot bring any expertise or skills to the business.
Your friend on the other hand would like your cash to help him expand the company and he does have the technical skills but lacks the money. You do have the cash, so you give the cash to your friend and in return, he gives you a legal share of the company, which means you own a % of his company.
As such you have purchased a stake in the business and that is an asset you now own in the exact same way you may purchase a property. That asset (share) is now an investment and you want that investment to perform. As you have invested directly in the business, your return on your investment is based directly on how well the business does. If the business does well and continues to make profits, you could expect to receive a dividend (share of the profits) and the value of your % share of the business should hopefully go up in value as the business does better and goes up in value itself. However if the business performs poorly and there are no profits, then there are no dividends. The value of your share may go down and if the business had other debts and subsequently fails, then the business may be forced to close and you lose everything.

The example I have described is actually the highest type of risk you can expose yourself to from investing in shares. Investing directly in a small start up company is extremely risky. The company can easily fail, you only need to check the UK statistics for how many start up firms close within the first four years, especially technical businesses as the market moves so quickly – remember the .com crash of 2000?

However if you had invested and owned 5% of Google, or Facebook or Amazon when they first started, you would be easily one of the richest people in the world right now. Finding the next Facebook is almost impossible so I would forget about searching for the next one, because you will come across many small technology firms all promising just that, many which never make it past year one.

What is less of a gamble and more of an investment is investing in 'blue chip' shares which are typically FTSE100 companies and as such make up the largest one hundred companies in the UK. These are typically large companies, which have been trading for many years, usually have a strong financial position and are unlikely to fail over night. That said and as mentioned previously, most of the major banks in the UK are FTSE100 companies and we know what happened in 2008. BP is also a long standing FTSE100 company of which many people and pension companies hold BP shares, but BP had a major problem with the oil spill in the gulf in 2010. So they are not entirely safe investments and still remain risky, but again offer the rewards of growth and Income from dividends.

What is viewed as less risky still, is to invest in a collective fund such as a Unit Trust (UT) or Open Ended Investment Company (OEIC). These are essentially pools of investor's money which is then invested on their behalf in a range of investments. This then spreads the risk across a number of shares or bonds which dilutes the threat of one company performing poorly or failing and as such spreads the risk. The trade off with this approach however is that it spreads the gains as well, so we typically see average gains and average losses in these funds compared to direct investment. However it is still deemed a risky investment. Again, we have to relate all this information back to you. What are your aims and goals from the investment? What is it that you want back in return and over what time scale? All of these factors play the determining role in what you should ultimately invest in. There is no silver bullet to investing and no one-size fits all. If that was the case everyone would be investing in the same things all the time, and that is not the case.

A very easy way to become an expert in investments is simple, focus on an industry or market sector which you know very well. For example if you work in the Insurance market you will probably have a good understanding about which insurers are doing well and which ones are doing poorly. You know that X insurer is writing lots of business and not suffering many losses, as a result it may be likely that when they announce their profits next year they could be much higher. Likewise you may be aware of which insurers are losing clients and suffering losses, it could be the case that their profits may be down when they next report?

As such you may choose to buy shares in the insurance company which is doing well. They may in fact not do well due to other factors, or they may as hoped, post great results, this usually has a positive effect on the shares and as such could make you a profit from investing in them. Warren Buffet always says stick to what you know and invest in what you understand. If you spend a lot of time on the internet you will probably be aware of new technology or social networking sites which are popular and doing well, as such they may be worth considering investing in. However if you know nothing about technology or modern trends in that area, it is probably best you stay well away!

Pensions

A personal pension is nothing more than a savings account. It's a special savings account into which you can pay money and receive a tax benefit for doing so.

Assuming you pay basic 20% tax and earn £100 pounds, you keep £80 after paying the £20 income tax. However if you then choose to pay that £80 into your pension, the government gives you back the £20 you paid in tax. Therefore paying money into a pension is tax free which is a huge benefit compared to other savings vehicles and also almost all the gains made within the pension are tax free also.

One of the drawbacks to a pension is once the money has been paid in, you cannot get it back (except in special circumstances) until you're at least 55 which is another potential drawback for someone who may need more flexibility. The pension is therefore seen as rather inflexible especially in recent years considering the vast changes in lifestyles and flexible living we have now become accustomed to.

Once the pension pot has grown and you reach retirement you can either, keep most of the money still in the pension and withdraw amounts that you need as and when you feel, or you can take all the money in the pension and purchase an annuity. This means that in return for all the money you have saved in your pension you swap for an annuity, usually from a major pensions or insurance provider who agree to pay you x amount per month/year as an income for life.

Because of the tax benefits it is very difficult to see why someone should not have a pension but clearly in the inflexibility does put some people off. You must try to not be short sighted but see the bigger picture and invest for the long term.

Pensions have had fairly bad press over the past few years based on pension performance and the relatively poor rates of annuities.

However the pension should have a place in everyone's retirement planning because if you don't take advantage of the tax benefits on offer, essentially you are in-part helping to fund everyone else's pension through the taxes you pay.

You should also seek to join your employer pension scheme if there is one available as they often come with additional linked benefits. There are changes coming to the UK in the coming years regarding pensions which should benefit people and help encourage further investment from savers and employers.

What I would encourage you to do now however is consider your retirement. I strongly believe that there is a looming pension's crisis to hit the UK in the next twenty years. People are not saving enough for retirement, people's expectations for their own lifestyle are very high, and the welfare society will not be around in its current form. Have a think about how much you will need in retirement? You hopefully will not have any mortgages or loans to repay so you simply need cash to live and maintain a standard of living. Do you think you will have a large pension 'pot' in the next twenty years? How much are you currently saving? I would seriously start giving it some consideration if I were you.

Nothing is more common than the sight of old people who yearn for retirement. And nothing is so rare than those who have retired and do not regret it.
(Saint-Evremond, 1610 - 1703)

Insurance & Protection

Insurance and Protection is something that doesn't need to be sold in the USA. People walk off the high street to see financial advisers and ask for protection insurance to cover their life, their income and family. The fact that they could die, be injured or out of work is a daily reality for most Americans and as such they are keen to ensure their family and lifestyle are protected.

In the UK, despite having the exact same risks, this is something which must be sold to people before they truly understand and appreciate the benefits on offer. This is because we have the NHS in the UK and the welfare state, something which they do not have in the USA. Because of this people in the UK tend to believe the state will provide for their health and wellbeing through sickness and health. We also have incapacity benefits and other state handouts which are provided to people should they fall on hard times or suffer some form of accident. In the USA they have no such reassurance and there is very much an attitude that you are responsible for yourself and your family.

The reality is that the state benefits in the UK are woefully small and provide only the very bare minimum amount of money to live on. It is more of an existence rather than a life. Based on the current times of austerity expect the amount of benefits to be smaller still. What few people truly understand is that if you die your family will not be looked after by the state. If you are in a serious accident and cannot work for a number of years, you're sick pay and state sick pay will not pay your bills, if you die there will be no one to provide an income to your partner or children, if you contract cancer tomorrow your company will not continue to pay you during therapy other than what is stated in your contract, and the mortgage company will still want paying. The world is not as kind as you hope and therefore YOU need to take precautions to ensure you and your loved ones will be taken care of should the worst happen – I assume that is a priority for you?

Speak to a financial adviser about the range of insurances and protection you can have to protect your family. Yes you hope you will not need them but don't view that as wasted money, because it is a price worth paying. For around £30 per month you can ensure your family receive a lump sum payout should you die to clear the mortgage and any other debts and provide additional cash. For a little more per month you can cover yourself against not being able to work due to accident or unemployment and for a little more still, you can provide an income upon death to see your kids through to their eighteenth birthday.

Consider your Category 3 payments. Would you swap £50 per month to Cable TV for complete piece of mind and assurance that your family will be taken care of in the event of your death? I would and I do.

Insurance and Protection needs to form a key part of your financial arrangements. Even if you cannot afford a large monthly amount, some protection is better than none. Speak to your independent financial adviser today.

Your own Business

Your own business is often seen by business owners as an asset however one which can be difficult to value. For example many business owners do not realise that they are often the businesses biggest asset, as such if they were to sell the business onto someone else, what is the value of the business without them – probably significantly less than with them.

That said, there are common accepted methods for valuing a business based on net asset values, multiple of incomes or value of existing client base, to name a few. If you can build your business, you will significantly increase the value of it by ensuring you are not part of the day to day running of it. Because of this it can be viewed as a standalone entity and as such the valuation can be justified with or without your involvement playing a factor.

A business can be seen as an asset aimed at future sale, after which you receive your capital invested. Obviously it can be a bumpy path along the way and you should be prepared for this and also the potential for the business to fail entirely, after which, you lose everything you have invested.

When you are running the business you have a few options as to what to do with the profits. You can essentially plough this money back into the business, invest for growth and drive the business. Alternatively you can withdraw the profits from the business in the most tax efficient way possible and invest this money elsewhere. The benefit to doing the latter is that if the business fails you have essentially got a lot of your cash out assuming you have limited your liability as a director. However the converse is true as if you do plough the money back into the company, the company will grow further and as such your asset is worth more. It's a tough choice and depends on how the business is performing. Remember despite the effort you put in, the business may still fail due to market factors or forces out of your control.

What tends to happen is that people start their own business out of passion or a desire for a certain lifestyle. Rarely do people start a business in something they have no interest in simply due to the earnings, you need to have drive or passion for your own business to start it and keep it going. Because of this our judgement can become clouded when making important business decisions. It may sound ruthless to consider extracting money from a business in case of failure, but it is the ruthlessness of mind you sometimes need in business.

Many business plans are created with an exit plan in mind. Therefore if you are planning to start your own business or currently run your own business, have you got an exit plan? My suggestion would be to consider one because without an exit strategy your business is only worth a fraction of what it could be worth with one.

Screw it, let's do it

I don't think of work as work, and play as play. It's all living

A business has to be involving, it has to be fun and it has to exercise your creative instincts

Richard Branson
(Branson)

Depreciation - what does it mean?

Do you really understand depreciation? I mean really understand it or is it simply a term you mention in the pub when talking about why things are worth less?
You need to understand depreciation as it is constantly working against you all the time to extract value from some of you things you own (your assets).

Have you ever been out and bought I brand new car? If the answer is yes then you're an idiot. I can say that because I have done the exact same thing, twice, both before the age of 22 and it was a stupid thing to do. The average car depreciation over the first 12 months is 40% according to the AA. This does vary from model to model but after one year, the car will be worth 40% of what you paid.
(The AA, 2010)

Now there are many factors which affect depreciation, some of which are out of your control. For example (keeping with the car theme) once the recession hit, large 4x4 vehicles became less popular due to the cost of running them and the rising price of petrol. You cannot control what the government will do to the rate of duty on fuel and you cannot control the oil cartel which is OPEC. Also fashion and trends can affect depreciation, for the example when the new Mini was launched they were so in-demand that you could sell one after 6 months for more than you paid for it brand new, due to the waiting list. This also shows us that depreciation is affected by supply and demand another factor out of your control.
What you can control however is what you do buy, how much you pay and what you do with it once you no longer want it.

Depreciation is so important because you should consider it whenever you buy something that will most likely re-sell on at a later date. See the section, 'What do you actually spend your money on' which relates to this topic regarding reselling items and offers a different mindset to owning and buying.

To highlight depreciation and the devastating affect it can have on your personal finance I will again use the example of purchasing a new car using simple figures.

- Vauxhall Insignia – RRP £19,350
- Personal Loan Tesco £19,400 over 4 years
- £475.13 per month @ 8.5%
- Total to be repaid £22,806

The Insignia's value	Outstanding Debt
After year 1: £10,875	£17,104
After year 2: £8,850	£11,403
After year 3: £7,150	£5,701.50
After year 4: £5,675	£0

So after 4 years you own the car outright and have an asset worth £5,675. It has cost you £22,806.

It has cost you £22,806 to buy an asset worth £5,675

If you sell the car after year four you have a net cost of £17,131 over four years. On average it has cost you £356 per month over 4 years.

Did you know you could have leased the same car over 4 years for £251.94 per month which would include road tax annually? You would have saved £104.35 per month which could have gone into your savings. Now running a car these days is expensive regardless of how you do it, however you should try and avoid owning an asset which is likely to depreciate significantly. If you prefer to own a car, buy a used one which has already lost its value. Cars are so well built these days, they are reliable and can go for many more years with minimal maintenance, get over the ego thing or the 'keeping up with the neighbours' and leave the new car purchase to others.

As you can see from the table, the moment you buy a brand new car, you immediately fall into negative equity (assuming you take a loan to purchase) which means you owe more than the asset is actually worth. For example if you wanted to sell the car after one year, you would owe £17,104 but only be able to see the car for £10,875, to clear the loan you would need to find an extra £6,229 – that is one measure of year 1 depreciation.

So how do you avoid depreciation? It's simple, only buy things that appreciate (go up in value) and not things which depreciate and go down in value. However in reality this not practical, as there are many items we need which will depreciate, such as computers, furniture, sports equipment, cars, electrical goods, white and brown goods and clothes. As a rule try and spend your money on things that go up in value (typically) such as property, shares, antiques, art, rare and classic cars, collectable items, stamps, land, coins and anything else you would expect to rise in value over time. I know we are running out of oil and they stopped making land a long time ago as well.
I am not saying never buy a new car again, it is your choice. If I had the money I would go out today and buy a brand new Ferrari, for the new car smell, prestige of being the first owner and getting the keys to a brand new car. You cannot beat that feeling and as such you need to consider how much you value that feeling and if it is worth paying. Remember it is your money and your choice but does it help you achieve your goals?

(Vauxhall UK, 2011)
(Tesco Finance, 2011)
(What Car, 2011)
(Nationwide Vechile Contracts, 2011)

Inflation - what does it mean?

Do you really understand inflation? I mean really understand it or is it simply a term you mention in the pub when talking about why things cost more?

The reality is this. Inflation is constantly working against your money, eroding its value so you can buy less and less with it. It is happening all the time, every second and you need to be constantly aware its affects. As I type inflation is currently running at 3.3% per annum so you need to protect your money against its terrible effects.

In the current climate we have a very strange situation where people who do not understand inflation are losing value in their money every day, when they actually think their savings are going up, let me explain.

HSBC Online Bonus Saver account: 0.75%
(Variable – meaning they can change it (up or down) should they wish)

However, before taking the account have we checked for inflation?

Currently inflation is running at 3.3% according to the Bank of England.

So what does this mean for our thrifty saver who opens the HSBC savings account (or any other banks saving account at the same rate)

- Assuming on January the 1st 2011, a new sofa costs exactly £500.
- On the same day you deposit £500 in your e-saver account at 0.75% and leave the money untouched for 12 months.
- During the course of the year inflation remains level at 3.3% throughout the entire year.

Assuming no other changes in taxation rates, 12 months later:
- The new sofa now costs £516.50
- Your savings are now worth £503.75
- You can no longer afford the sofa
- There is a difference of £12.75 between the cost of the sofa & your savings

This example shows clearly, at the start of the year you could buy the sofa outright using the cash you have in your hand. If you decide to save at an interest rate that is lower than inflation, then your savings are going down in value in real terms. Don't forget unless the savings are within an ISA, or if you have used up your ISA limit or depending on your tax position, then the interest on your savings could also be subject to tax and this will reduce your total savings even further.

The crucial thing to remember is this. If the rate on your savings is less than inflation, then your money is going down in value and is worth less in real terms. Your paying power is shrinking as things are becoming more expensive at a quicker rate than your savings are growing at. You need to find a rate on your savings that is above inflation to ensure your savings stay ahead and don't go down in value in real terms.

If money does not bring you happiness, it will at least help you be miserable in comfort

(Brown H. G.)

(HSBC, 2011)
(Bank of England, 2011)
Figures correct as of 15th Jan 2011

What do you actually spend your money on?

So now we have looked at inflation and depreciation, let's think about what you actually spend your money on.

We have already said that a detailed budget is useless on a daily basis, but it is a worthwhile exercise to create a detailed budget of your monthly outgoings to give you some perspective on exactly what you spend your money on and then make a plan.

For example that newspaper, sandwich and the Starbucks you buy for lunch may only be costing you only £7.60 per day, however that could be £1,500 per year, that's the price of a holiday! Although this book is not about penny pinching, you do have to be aware of where the money goes each day, week and month.

Buy once and buy well is one of my favourite sayings. My wife comes home at weekend with bags of shopping containing a large number of garments. Before I launch into a rage about how much they cost, she quickly explains that each item was only £5 or £6 or only £12 so it is all very cheap. The reality is that due to the price being low, she simply bought more items so in real terms she has not spent any less from going to the cheaper store, she just bought more things! However I will simply buy just one quality well made polo-shirt. Why? Because it will fit better, wash well, last longer and be a recognised brand of quality. Even better for me, I don't have to trawl around shops, as I know what I like and what suits me, so I just stick to what I know.

E-bay (and other web based auction sites) are a fantastic resource and you should start using it for things you no longer need. Big companies spend millions advertising every year to get their products and services in front of large numbers of customers. You can sell your items on E-bay and get access to millions of customers worldwide in one place for a tiny fee.

The beauty of this mass-market is that you get access to everyone and that includes the dim-wits who don't know the value of items and will pay far more than they should for your used items. If you plan to sell your items in future on E-bay, you can take this into consideration when you buy items.

I bought a mountain bike three years ago. I was new to the sport and most people would have bought an entry level bike, which is cheaper and made of basic equipment. I didn't, I bought a Trek which is one of the best bikes which also came with lots of additional extras. I paid £600 for the bike. I sold the bike 3 years later for £230 on E-bay.

Therefore the bike had only cost me £370 in real terms, I had the use of a high spec bike for 3 years and I was able to sell it once I no longer wanted it.

Had I purchased an entry level bike, and let's assume it would have cost £350, because it was a low spec bike, it may have required repair or maintenance more often, crucially I would have struggled to sell the bike to anyone because who wants a low spec second hand bike?

Therefore it's worth considering the value of an item when you purchase it, ask yourself, can I sell this on, would it still be desirable in 2 years from now, is there a second hand market for this item. You can view your purchases as investments, your tying up part of your money in an item, some of which you will get back in the future. Try and consider this approach when purchasing any items of value and consider it as an investment. So look after the things you buy and be aware of what is happening in the world regarding demand for your possessions, if you are really smart, you may even make a profit.

Opportunity Cost

Whenever you are making any decision about what to do with your money, you should always be considering the opportunity cost.

The opportunity cost is something we often consider in business when deciding what a company should do with its cash. For example let's say company A produces £100,000 in profit. What should it do with the profit? It could hire more staff and acquire bigger premises. This may produce a return on the £100k of 15%. But what if the company can get 18% return by investing the £100,000 in financial investments? Rather than grow the core business, it may actually be more financially beneficial to invest the cash in either stocks or bonds. For the shareholders of the business, they may prefer this as the best use of company assets and what will achieve the best return on investment (ROI).

That may be a wise choice especially in times of uncertainty, that said, some may say that's the best time to invest in the business and grow it further which may not give you the 18% ROI but it could be argued it will increase the value of the business overall and raise the price of shareholders shares and overall provide a greater return over the long term.

The point is that there are always different options as to what to do with your money and a cost associated with it. Opinions will always differ as to what is the best thing to do with your cash amongst the many forms of investment that exist out there. You should therefore keep in mind the opportunity cost of other options available to you. What you can find yourself doing however is endlessly examining different options without coming to any sort of decision, which brings us nicely onto the next chapter.

Cost of delay

Cost of delay in investing terms is the loss of gains you could have made from investing sooner. We often see this calculation when considering starting a pension. We can show that for every year you delay starting your pension, what the negative impact will be on your pension on retirement. The closer you are to retirement, the greater the effect. We can calculate the shortfall which needs to be made up through higher pension contributions for each year delayed.

In all forms of investment there are costs to delay. For example if the stock market is rising quickly, waiting another week before investing means you may miss out on some of the greatest gains that year. Often we hear that the best things come to those that wait, however you only get the leftovers from those that hustle.

That said, the 'cost' associated to delay can often be a price worth paying if it means you avoid an unfavourable investment and one which could have lost you money. The cost of delay is always a secondary factor when considering an investment as thought, research and consideration must all come first.

The cost of delay can be calculated over many different time scales. For example when considering the cost of delay in stock market investing could be measured in minutes. The cost of delay from starting a pension could be measured over forty years. The cost of delay from getting on the property ladder could be measured over months. It is all relative to you and your chosen investment, but it is something which should be factored in.

The other measure for cost of delay can be the delay in disposing of a loss making or depreciating asset. Many people make investment mistakes by holding onto an asset rather

than selling it and taking a loss in hope that it will come good. The reason why is, emotionally speaking, we sometimes cut the flowers and water the weeds.
This means we often see people taking a profit too soon rather than letting it grow and make further profits over time. And conversely we often see people making the mistake of holding on too long when an investment is going down in hope it will turn into profit. When it comes to investing, in all its forms, you need to learn when to take loss, because if you don't take small losses, one day you will take the mother of all losses and the fat lady will be more than just warmed up.

Like many things already mentioned in this book it comes down to discipline and emotional intelligence. For example, look at how many people smoke on a daily basis. Of these people how many actually are aware of the damage smoking causes? The reality is most of them are fully aware of the damage they are doing to their throat, mouth, lungs, heart because we are developed and highly evolved species and we are educated about our own health and well being. So why do they continue to do it? They could stop tomorrow but they choose not to. They would need to be strong and stop, but they don't. It is exactly the same principle when it comes to investing.

Respect your efforts, respect yourself. Self-respect leads to self-discipline.
When you have both firmly under your belt, that's real power
(Eastwood)

Return on Investment (ROI)

Whatever you do decide to do with your money, this is the question you need to be asking yourself. Any shrewd investor always asks, what is in it for me?

Just because your parents think putting your money in the bank is a good idea, you don't have to agree regardless. Think about it, weigh up the options, find out what you are comfortable with, but most of all work out what your return on investment will be, because if the plan is to grow your investment, this is the measure we must use.

ROI is often measured in percentage terms and is an expression of what we get back based on how much we have invested. The bigger the percentage, the better.

But the ROI can be difficult to calculate and therefore difficult to ensure you have calculated it correctly. Most financial investments will come with previous performance statistics which show past performance. This of course is no guide to how the investment will perform in the future, but gives us a form guide to the performance of the fund manager over previous years which can offer reassurance.

Everyone will have their own opinion regarding past performance, we know the FSA's opinion as they insist on risk warnings accompanying anything which relates to previous performance.

My thoughts are, form is temporary and class is permanent. Fernando Torres has just signed for £50m for Chelsea. He has played a few games but is yet to score a goal, but he is still a world class striker and that is something to consider when it comes to choosing investment funds.

Risk

Learn to love this one because there is never any getting away from risk in all its forms in everyday life. It is even more prevalent in the world of finance.

Some people enjoy risk and like the exposure to uncertainty because they see it as a challenge and something that is fun. Some people are terribly fearful of Risk and don't want any exposure to it.

The problem with Risk was summed up by Del Boy rather nicely. He who dares, wins!

That is because Risk is always associated with uncertainty and anyone who reads the financial press will know that the financial markets do not like uncertainty. The very definition of Risk is summed up by Wikipedia:

Risk is the potential that a chosen action or activity (including the choice of inaction) will lead to a loss (an undesirable outcome).

The most important word in this definition is 'potential' and in there lies the uncertainty which many of us do not like.
Risk is relative to our circumstances. Billionaires can happily invest a few million in a risky start up venture as they can afford to lose a few million without significantly impacting on their finances or quality of life.
For someone investing £20,000 which is the accumulation of a lifetime's saving, then they will have an entirely different approach to how they invest that money.

Risk cannot be controlled but it can be managed. You can control your exposure to risk but you cannot completely eradicate it from all equations. Risk can be managed by having a structured approach to the amount of risk you expose yourself to. For example, our chap with £20,000 to invest can take a structured approach and create a portfolio for his

£20,000. He can choose to invest 90% of his money in very low risk (and as such low return) investments and expose just 10% of his wealth to riskier investments.

The thinking behind this that should the 10% investment result in a total loss, the 90% proportion of the investment will make up for this with hopefully some small surplus.
However should the 10% proportion produce a great return then the investor has made money and the 90% proportion will have grown also. The investor can then cash in the 10% proportion along with the gains and move them into the less risky 90% proportion. The investor can then keep repeating this process again and again and so the circle continues.

This is just one example of how you can control your exposure to risk. There are much more complicated model portfolios where you can further 'blend' your exposure to risk across the risk spectrum. What I can say is many wealthy people rarely become so without taking a risk at some point. He who dares, wins Rodney!

The crucial element in risk management is you. You must be fully aware of the risk, the potential for losses and the potential gains and knowing your potential total loss. As long you are comfortable with the decisions you make, enjoy the fun of the fair!

The person who risks nothing, does nothing, has nothing, is nothing and becomes nothing. He may avoid suffering and sorrow but he simply cannot learn and feel and change and grow and love and live
(Buscaglia, 1924 - 1998)

Man cannot discover new oceans unless he has the courage to lose sight of the shore
(Gide, 1869 - 1951)

Good Debt & Bad debt

There are two types of debt, good debt and bad debt. If you have not read Rich Dad, Poor Dad (Kiyosaki, 2002) yet, I would recommend it as that book covers this point very well.

In simple terms, have a look at the application form for a personal loan from a bank. They ask a variety of questions, one of which is "what is the purpose of the loan?"
The options are, holiday, new car, home improvement, debt consolidation etc. Do they ever have an option for starting a business, investing in shares, joint business venture or building property empire? The answer is no.

Banks are very happy to lend you money for holidays and cars, TV's and computers, items which go down in value, but banks won't lend to you to buy or invest in something which could make you richer. Banks offer bling-bling debt to spend on an experience or something which will depreciate. Before I start bank bashing I will say they will often lend for home improvements which can be argued will appreciate over time and could be viewed as an investment. However as a rule they do not offer good debt – or at least they are much more reluctant to do so and charge you a higher premium for the privilege.

For example now, if you want to buy a property to rent out, the mortgage rate and charges will be significantly more for a buy-to-let mortgage than they would be for a mortgage to purchase a home to live in via a residential mortgage. A commercial loan is much more expensive than a personal loan, that's why many small businesses start off with the owner re-mortgaging their own house or taking out a personal loan to get the business started. Even if a small business did take a commercial loan, the banks normally want personal guarantees from the directors anyway, meaning they are essentially personally liable for the loan after the business.

The view regarding debt should not be that all debt is bad, in actual fact debt can be a fantastic tool to make you wealthy. However many people will tell you to stay clear of debt, don't borrow, but it is they who are really missing a trick.

Borrow money for things which will make you money – that's as plain and simple as I can put it. Borrow to start a business that will make you profit. Borrow to buy a property that will give you rent and capital appreciation. Borrow to buy that very rare item which can be sold for a profit in years to come. Borrow to pay for qualifications that will result in you getting a better job and greater earning power. Borrow to make improvements to your home that will increase its value. If you have to borrow then borrow for these reasons as this is a good form of debt to repay, borrow to invest. This way the debt pays for itself and should then provide an additional return.

However it is not without risk, for example if you borrow money to start a business which ultimately fails, then you are still liable for the loan. But is that any different than borrowing £5,000 for a dream holiday? After 2 weeks all you have are the pictures and the memories, but you still have a debt to repay? Better to have tried and failed, than failed to try. What you must do is stay clear of the bad debt. Holidays, cars, clothes, household goods and furniture – try to avoid borrowing to purchase these items. Try and also pay cash as there is nothing more depressing for the soul than seemingly making endless repayments for something you own, 4 years after you bought it, which you no longer want and are already planning to replace. It's a dark place, don't go there.

Don't tell me where your priorities are. Show me where you spend your money and I will tell you what they are
(Frick, 1923 - 2008)

Penny pinching is not a strategy

Part of taking an active approach to improving your life is about making changes which will have a positive effect on your life. Getting your finances in order is definitely a positive step and should make you feel good, however that is assuming that penny pinching is not your intended method.
Saving money is a good thing but not to the extent that you count every penny and are afraid to spend money. Don't count every penny. As mentioned earlier do your budget once and make a plan. Calculate how much you can spend per month and stick to it, get into a routine. Try and keep some small luxuries as you are more likely to stick to a plan which offers some small reward rather than a strict plan which offers nothing.

That said you will be pleasantly surprised by just how much money you can save over a few months by simply cutting down on your spending. I have already mentioned previously how these savings can be made, but try and keep those little treats. Try and make your saving visual if possible. I mentioned earlier about the jars I have in the office, get some jars and put the money in there when you come home every day. They soon start to fill up with your small savings. My local bank branch has a coins machine into which you can pour all your coins into, it automatically counts them and totals the amount, then deposits this amount direct into your bank account. A friend of mine cashed all his jars in just before Christmas and encouraged me to do the same. However I will not do it. Not because I have become attached to the jars but simply the visual incentive they give me every day to continue saving. Penny pinching is not fun nor is it enjoyable and it is not a strategy. It will make you feel miserable and it rarely is a successful in its aims.

Money will buy you a fine dog, but only love can make its tail wag
(Friedman)

49

Do without, be disciplined!

This is a very simple one. It comes down to discipline again but it is simply a case of don't buy things you don't need. I know it can be difficult but stick with it and keep on top of things. You will be amazed how you can go an entire week and keep that £10 note still in your wallet. Just be strong. If you have had a long drive back from a meeting, you don't have to stop at motorway services for an expensive, over priced coffee, stick it out till you get home and have a homemade brew. Simple example but you get the point. Just because it is Friday you don't have to have the breakfast roll, just do your usual thing. My other favourite is the pay-day treats, notice how people treat themselves to extra treats around pay day and then spend the rest of the month scrimping to get by, not good.

I have decided to give up drinking beer for the new-year. Originally the plan was to quit just for January but we are well into February and I am still going strong. I have had the odd pint, but otherwise I am free of it and feel so much better for it, I suggest giving it a try. I didn't drink a lot and rarely went to the pub unless there was a big game on the TV to watch. What I did do was call at the supermarket on Friday afternoon and buy a week's worth of drink. This would consist of 2 bottles of wine and 8 bottles of beer which in total would cost around £15. In the six weeks since I quit I have saved £90 which can be put to better use rather than damaging my liver. It also means I don't have a sore head on Saturday or Sunday morning and therefore can get more things done at weekend. So I certainly suggest giving this one a try, or at least cutting right down. Trust me when I say, you will feel so much better after the first few weeks, more money in your pocket, much healthier and slimmer!

There is another way of looking at this which seems less extreme but just as effective. You make an effort to reduce your spending as an ongoing concern. How do you do this?

Well start with the simple things, skip the posh expensive coffee and get a brew in the office. Don't go for the expensive lunch and just grab a sandwich from the local shop. Do you really need that new shirt or will the existing ones continue to do fine? This sounds like penny pinching but it isn't, its sensible money management, your still spending money – you not starving yourself, simply reducing the amount you spend on everyday items.

There are many different ways you can do this, but think about your everyday life and think about what changes you can make. It is not penny pinching but it is discipline and thought for what you are spending and they are two entirely different things.

Be disciplined, keep it up and you will be very surprised how much you save in only a few months.

The art is not in making money, but in keeping it
(Unknown)

When I was young I thought that money was the most important thing in life, now that I am old I know that it is
(Wilde, 1854-1900)

Of the billionaires I have known, money just brings out the basic traits in them. If they were jerks before they had money, they are simply jerks with a billion dollars
(Buffet)

Do NOT spend what you earn

The one thing I see time and again, is people tend to spend every penny they earn and the one thing which makes this fact true is that, the more people earn - the more they spend.

Not true I hear you say, but sorry it's only too true and I have seen it so many times. Often our clients need to provide bank statements to us as part of a mortgage application and as such we get see peoples spending habits, what they earn, when and how they spend their money. Do you know anyone who has recently had a promotion or pay rise? How did you find out? Was it because they bought a bigger car? New conservatory? Did they have an exotic holiday? Did they suddenly have a season ticket at Old Trafford? Are you starting to see my point? We are all guilty of this at some point and I include myself in that.

We can all be guilty of this at some point, and it goes someway to explaining why the UK has the savings problem that other European countries do not. We as individuals don't save enough compared to our European cousins and we are all too quick to pull out the credit card as well. I genuinely feel a large correction is coming for UK individuals who simply do not save enough nor pay into a pension. As such as the population grows and becomes older, anyone who is relying on the state to increase benefits, handouts and state pensions to elderly people are going to be sadly disappointed. Speak with an adviser sooner rather than later about sorting out your savings and pensions.

Who is richer?
A Solicitor earning £80,000 per year or a teacher earning £30,000? The answer is the teacher. Why? Because after the Solicitor has paid his huge mortgage payment, his Porsche & Range Rover finance, paid for the cleaner and the child care, paid for his skiing holiday and Caribbean break as well as a few

golf weekends. After the golf, gym, and football membership, his left over 'disposable' income is £4,000.

The teacher has £4,500 disposable after his commitments. He doesn't spend as much as the Solicitor and that's why he is richer. The solicitor has a higher income but also has higher commitments and as such net wealth is not as great as the teacher. Now yes, the solicitor could easily cancel the gym membership or take one less golf break and probably has more in assets, but I hope you see the point.

Now let's assume the Solicitor is in a car accident coming home one day from work and can no longer work due to severe injuries and has not bothered to take out any form of insurance to protect against such an event. His life as he knows it is finished overnight, because he spends what he earns, if he doesn't earn he cannot spend and the life style ends. What you should aim to do is build a sustainable life style based on current and future earnings. It may mean you don't go out and buy the Porsche right now, but delay it for a few years. Save more of your income and invest it. Get your money working for you, you don't want to always be working for money.

Think about it this way. Would you like to have no mortgage? For those that own their own home will have almost certainly bought it with a mortgage and as such my guess is this is your single largest monthly outgoing? Would it be nice if you didn't have this payment and how would that affect your monthly income and outgoings? You could live your life differently. You wouldn't need to do the job you have to do for the money, you could instead do a job you love for a less money and still live comfortably. You wouldn't feel chained to a 25 year commitment and feel free to move or change your circumstances? You could perhaps raise a larger family and don't forget, you would now have a very valuable asset which you owned outright. A nice thought I am sure you will agree.

So why not pay off your mortgage tomorrow? You cannot, it is too large, but let us look at it in more detail.

Let us assume you are Mr Average (sorry, you are actually very special) and as Mr Average you live in the average value house, have the average size mortgage and earn the average salary. As such:

- You earn   £24,000
- Your mortgage amount is   £130,971
- Your house is worth   £246,387

Without going into lots of detailed calculations, you could pay off your mortgage in just over 6 years. Six years of hard graft and the mortgage is gone. How does that sound?

Ah yes, all very well, but that assumes I don't spend a penny of the money I earn - I hear you say. Well yes that's true. All the same let us imagine you do this and save every penny to repay the mortgage. How will you live? Well could you in theory live off your partner's income? Could you in theory get a part-time job working weekends or evenings which would provide a living? Could you start a business working from home or an e-bay business? Ok if that's a little extreme, what if your part time job provides the majority of your earnings and you used a little of the income from your main income? You may still have the mortgage paid in 7 or 8 years?

This is an extreme example but it could be done this way. Live like a monk for 7 years then have complete freedom from your mortgage for the rest of your life? It is not the worst deal ever is it?

I am not advocating you do this, but I hope the extreme example perhaps gets your mind thinking about possible other ways you could do this?

(Office of National Statistics, 2011)
(Your Mortgage.co.uk, 2011)

Grow rich slowly

Getting rich slowly is sustainable and therefore recommended. It also is a process which will naturally breed self-discipline and prudence.

You may see adverts on the internet about get rich quick schemes. They do not exist so please don't be fooled by them. They do not exist so please don't be fooled by them (it is not a print error, I typed it twice).

With time comes experience, judgement, awareness, knowledge and understanding. I am sure you will agree, these are good qualities to have when managing money – especially when it is your own. The reality is that unless you are prepared to take large risks with your own cash and risk losing all of it - potentially, then the stratospheric returns you crave are not going to happen.

That said, the more risk you are prepared to take, then the higher potential returns. My advice would be to take a balanced approach and spread your investments.

For example if you choose to invest on a monthly basis then take a five year approach and invest with a financial adviser in a spread of different funds. Some funds will be cautious and others can be adventurous depending on your attitude to risk and tolerance to loss. However you don't spread your investment equally across the funds, as such you could have 80% of your money in cautious funds and take more of a risk on the remaining 20% of your funds. Your adviser should check this every few months to ensure your balance stays at 80/20 and will move money from one area to another to ensure it stays balanced.

You may also consider investing directly in shares. Now this is often viewed as very high risk on the risk'o'meter however I don't think that is the case at all. Read any of Warren Buffets books on how to invest and you will see that Warren has become one of the wealthiest people on the planet from investing directly in shares. He doesn't do hundreds of calculations, read thousands of charts and monitors computers screen 24 hours per day. He looks at the fundamentals of the business, is it well run, do they have a good financial position, are they in a market which has growth or do they have a niche in that market. So basically as long as you keep up to date with the news, have a broad understanding of what is going on in the economy then you should fair ok investing in an industry you understand.

For example the share price of UK banks is very low and has been for a number of years. Once we know what the UK government plans to do regarding breaking up of the banks, they probably will look a decent investment in the future. We need banking, the banks seem to have done the reforms required since the credit crunch and will probably grow steadily over the next five years with plenty of ups and downs along the way.

Please note the above information does not represent a recommendation to invest and as such, the author accepts neither liability nor blame in any form, from any investment decisions you make upon reading this book. See the chapter 'Stop moaning, get on with it & don't blame others' for additional information.

Someday I want to be rich. Some people get so rich they lose all respect for humanity. That's how rich I want to be
(Rudner)

Every day I get up and look through the Forbes list of the richest people in America. If I'm not there, I go to work
(Orben)

They say it is better to be poor and happy than rich and miserable, but how about a compromise like moderately rich and just moody?
(Diana)

56

Don't be a great payer & always haggle

You don't have to the best payer when it comes to business costs or any other bills which don't appear on your credit file. If they DO appear on your credit file then you must keep payments up to date to maintain your credit rating, I have mentioned previously about the importance of maintaining your credit score.

However for expenses relating to your business or anything else, don't be so keen to give others your money. You should always be asking for additional time to pay and never offering to pay a premium for doing so. You should always be cheeky in asking for this and also trying to negotiate down the price of everything you buy. It's not being tight with your money, it is just business and business is about profit and you want to maximise yours.

What you should also do is haggle for everything, if nothing else it's good fun! Worst case you have some banter with suppliers and best case you have some banter and you save some money, so its win-win.
You should also do this in your personal life. I bought a new door yesterday and I asked for a discount off the price because I felt the door was not in pristine condition. The retail price was £105 and I ended up paying £65 which I felt was a great price. The saving I made basically paid for the door handles and hinges!

You may hear people say things such as, the rich stay rich, because they don't spend any money! I don't think that is the case, they just get value for money and are not too proud to ask for a discount.

A bank will lend you money if you can prove you do not need it
(Hope)

Manage Your Life

Self- Delayed Gratification & Discipline

For me, my approach to life is about self discipline, seeing the bigger picture and patience. This alone is what will make you far wealthier and successful than anything else in the long term.

We all have dreams. But in order to make dreams into reality, it takes an awful lot of determination, dedication, self-discipline, and effort (Owens, 1913 - 1980)

We want to have dreams and goals, but we also need to impose some discipline in terms of how we achieve them. For example many people may say they want to own a Ferrari before the age of 30. That's fine if you can afford to buy it in a sustainable way. However if you need to go out and take out a large loan to buy it then your only fooling yourself and probably ignoring some fundamentals in order to impress others or yourself. There is not much point having a Ferrari if its parked every night on the street and you have to stay in every night looking at it because you cannot afford to go out. You don't see many Ferraris parked outside a flat in the rough part of town – or maybe you do and that's my point.

I am a big advocate of long term sustainable investment in all its forms. Invest in yourself, invest financially and invest in your future. See the bigger picture and where you see yourself in the next 10 years, is what you are doing now ensuring you are on the road to getting there? Is what you did today ensuring you are going directly towards the destination? Did you decide to go out shopping today instead of putting that money into your savings? If so are you on track or have you put yourself back by one month? Only you know the answer and most importantly you're playing by your rules, you're the referee, the player and the manager all at the same time.

You can decide to give in and break the rules, they are your rules you are breaking and there is no one there to stop you.

Is there a god? Well I don't know, but I know lots of people pray to a god of some sort and it can be argued that people and society actually take comfort in the thought of a higher being. The thought that there is a higher being looking over us and someone who has created some rules and standards for us to live by seems to fill some psychological need in all of us. And despite what people say about freedom, trust me people need rules, routine and direction in work and life. Societies need laws otherwise there would be chaos. Children need discipline to learn rules and teach them right from wrong, and successful people have discipline and governance over their time and attitude towards work and life.

As such your discipline and rules regarding your finances and your life are created solely by you. If you break them you're only cheating yourself and making the whole process redundant at the same time.
That is where discipline comes into all of this. You have to stick to the course and show restraint as temptation is always just around the corner, ready to destroy all your well laid plans. How are your new year's resolutions coming along or did they drop off the radar during the third week of January?

Don't be a flash in the pan, a bright spark that soon burns out, flavour of the month or someone who clings onto something great they did many years ago. Instead be the real deal, be the one who genuinely makes a difference every single day, week in-week out, don't do one-offs to impress others, do things everyday for yourself, because you're the one who will be there at the end of the journey, no one else, so be true to yourself.

By constant self-discipline and self control you can develop greatness of character

(Kleiser, 1868 - 1953)

Stop moaning, get on & don't blame others!

This is one of the main areas I really take issue with. I have seen so many people make the choice of restricting their own progression in life due to their attitude with the world. You know the sorts, the ones who say it can never be done, you need luck to get ahead, you need money to make money, and you are wasting your time because that has already been done.

They think they are experts on every subject and yet have achieved nothing themselves. Because their life has not gone as planned, they do not think anyone else's should, at least that is their mind set. They blame everyone else for anything they are unhappy with. They think there is a cosmic imbalance in the universe where everything should be equal and people who get ahead in life are just 'lucky' or it is 'unfair' and that they are victims in some way for having no luck.

Most people miss Opportunity because it comes dressed in overalls and looks like work.

(Edison, 1847 - 1931)

The reality is simple. You are the driver, navigator and captain on the journey of your life. I can also tell you that it will never be the perfect time to start your own business, it is never the right time to start a family, you will never have enough time to attend that course, you will always think about renting for another 6 months before buying and you will never have enough money to save or invest in that idea.

It is never the perfect time, because the perfect time doesn't exist, all we have is now - because the future is always tomorrow.

You will not encounter any signposts on the journey of your life, there are no pre-recorded messages to guide you, and there are no maps. It is your life and your journey. Therefore you have to chart the map, plot the course, plan the route and drive the car to the destination all by yourself plus baggage – and there will be some baggage. Sorry – no sat nav!

Therefore manage your own expectations and do it sooner rather than later. Be prepared for the journey. The people who moan that life is not fair are the ones who simply have not prepared for their journey. They are the ones who have got a flat tyre on the journey and are expecting others to stop and help, they don't realise they have to help themselves. Instead they stand on the side of road watching others go past and complaining. They moan that other people get ahead, that they have no luck and everyone else is fortunate.

When you drive past these people on your journey, put your foot down and keep going. Don't listen to them, they are the energy vampires and the doom merchants, don't let them hold you back and infect your mind with their negativity. They are constantly recruiting new members, they do not like being on their own, and its easy when you have suffered some misfortunate to join their team of naysayers. Do not do it. Drive past, don't listen and keep true to your route and destination because these guys for certain, are going nowhere.

So stop moaning and start doing. Stop focusing on the problems and start thinking about solutions, because time is ticking and it waits for no man. So start planning your journey today and remember you are on your own, but take good advice when you can get it….oh and keep reading this book as well!

The golden opportunity you are seeking is in yourself. It is not in your environment, it is not in luck or chance, or the help of others, it is in yourself alone

(Marden, 1850 - 1924)

Manage your own Expectations

You are in charge of your own destiny and as such you are charting the course and making the decisions, therefore you should know best about how you are doing. You should know how you are getting along and if you are behind, on, or ahead of your target.

So if that is the case why do people get upset, disappointed, over-excited, depressed or delighted? Often it is because they are not constantly and actively managing their expectations.

You need to manage your own expectations, that way you are better able to handle any major surprises along the way. Now life will throw many unexpected events your way – but managing these is about managing your emotions and emotional intelligence.

I am talking about managing your expectations. Managing your own expectations is about setting an internal measure by which you can benchmark against.

If you start your own business and you do not become a millionaire by the end of the week, are you right to feel aggrieved by this? No, not at all as that would be an unrealistic expectation. Should you automatically assume your business will fail after the first week? Again no, as this is an unrealistic expectation. So who sets your expectations? You do.

Therefore it is your responsibility to manage them and you do this through experience and knowledge i.e. knowing what to expect, and when you are lacking in experience, you do what you should always do, go get good advice.

Speak to people more experienced than you when starting a new venture and ask them what can you realistically expect from your efforts? If you have done it all before then you should know how to manage your expectations, as you will know what to expect!

What you will find over time is that if you can manage your own expectations you will avoid and eliminate the rollercoaster that are emotions and be more composed, level headed, rational and thoughtful in your approach to life and business. Although you will not have x-ray vision into the future you will have a better understanding of the likelihood of events allowing you to plan better. You will not of course get it right every time, but for every time you get it wrong, you have even more experience to recall on for the future. Managing your expectations is not about visualising a fixed outcome. It is about constantly managing them and updating them based on your circumstances, the environment you are in and external factors outside of your control.

The outcome of good expectation management will mean you are less likely to get frustrated, angry or despondent. You are more likely to go the distance and see your plans through. You are more likely to stick the course and continue what you are doing because broadly speaking, your results should be in-line with expectations, and that is where you want to be. You will then start to laugh at others when you hear complaints such as 'I can't believe that' 'I wasn't expecting that' and 'Nothing ever goes my way' because you are actively managing your expectations.

Anger always comes from frustrated expectations
(Larson)

Keep high aspirations, moderate expectations and small needs
(Stein)

Disappointment is a sort of bankruptcy – the bankruptcy of a soul that expends too much in hope and expectation
(Hoffer)

Manage other people's expectations

This relates to what I have said about owning the agenda in discussions, meetings, and in business and life.

If you are managing other people's expectations, then to a certain degree, you can control their future reactions and emotions. More importantly you can control their thoughts and feelings towards you. It can be very powerful and it can give you serious influence over others. But please do not mistake influence for power or control, as they are different things and we simply want to influence by managing their expectations – you are not Darth Vader using the dark side of the force!

For example, let us say you use the old classic trick of UPOD, (Under Promise - Over Deliver). You tell the boss that the job will take you at least three weeks and cost £1,000. However after one week, you tell the boss the job is complete and it only cost £600. Wow, the boss will be impressed, you have saved her £400 and also done the job two weeks earlier. But is that the real story?

What if the job was only ever a one week job in the first place and you were not particularly busy with other things, and the cost was simply an over estimation on your part? What is the net result? You have done a job that had to be done, which you always had to do and you have done it in the normal time expected and done so for the typical cost. The boss is very happy with the cost and time savings and thinks you are a great worker! Everyone is happy and all because you pre-prepared the expectations of the boss, you didn't do anything different from a work perspective.

Ok so this a very simple example but hopefully this illustrates my point. Obviously you cannot do the same thing every time as the boss will remember how long the job should take and cost next time round, but you see the point.

Managing people's expectations is not about wild over exaggerations and constantly doing things quicker, cheaper, faster. It is about being realistic with other people but ensuring they are fully informed to be able to form their own expectations as well. Except for the information you give them and how you deliver it, can have a massive impact on how they form their own expectations of you.
It is in this area that you have some 'play' to allow their expectations to form in a manner deemed more favourable for you – and that's never a bad thing.

There are some very simple methods to do this. For example whenever the boss or anyone else asks how things are, just be positive in your summary and don't mention any negatives. You will be amazed by the impression you leave on others as they will always associate a positive impression with you.
UPOD is a very simple one, but I use it all the time in many different forms, it's a classic and they often work the best.
If you need something from someone, never go to them with the problem alone. Always go to them with the problem and your idea for the solution. By doing this, their expectations of you will be of someone who is capable of generating their own solutions to problems, even if you are not always right.

The one thing to be wary of however is raising expectations too high – that can be dangerous and you can set yourself up for a massive fall, you have been warned!

When ones expectations are reduced to zero, one really appreciates everything one does have

(Hawking)

Become the master of time

Time management is one of the most misunderstood and understated of all skills. So many times I have heard people say they have no time, believing that is the issue – the reality is that complaining about having no time, is in fact the symptom of poor time management.

Half our life is spent trying to find something to do with the time we have rushed through life trying to save.
(Rogers, 1879 - 1935)

It should be a simple thing to manage and it is, in isolation. However we do not live our lives in isolation or a vacuum, we live our lives in a very busy world which imposes massive demands on our time, constantly. Think about your plan for the day (I assume you make a plan for your day every morning?) how often is the plan executed to perfection – the answer is never. Oh and it is not your fault is it? No, it is everyone else's fault because John from accounts had to have a chat with you today and admin needed to clarify your travel plans for next Tuesday. You were invited out to lunch with your client and you could not say no, that piece of business landed on your desk and became priority number one, what else could you do? It is not your fault, is it?

The answer is simple, take control and manage your time, prioritise your work, make sacrifices and be courteous with people and ruthless with time. That's all you have to do and everyday will run like clockwork – literally.

Take control because your time is your time. So treat it preciously as you only get 24 hours in a day, so use them wisely. You don't get anymore or any less hours than everyone else. Therefore be ruthless with this most precious of all resources and ensure every second is spent on achieving your goals. However be courteous with people, so when John from

66

accounts simply must speak with you, offer alternative times, suggest another day or explain your situation and see if he can compromise, you don't have to be rude about it and other people will understand.

Often I hear people say "I cannot do this because X has asked me to do this" simple, learn to say NO. Be courteous with people and ruthless with time. So say "sorry but I cannot do this because I am busy with other things which must take priority" don't worry, people will understand. If it is the boss asking you to do something, then you cannot say no, but explain what the fallout will be by postponing the work you are currently doing. That way, the boss can then decide and push the decision back on them.

I will not continue anymore with this subject as I could write an entire book on the subject. Practice the basics and if you don't have time, just make some!

Time is free, but it is priceless. You cannot own it, but you can use it. You cannot keep it, but you can spend it. Once it is lost, you never get it back
(Mackay)

Don't count every hour in the day, make every hour in the day count
(Unknown)

Don't say you do not have enough time. You have exactly the same number of hours per day that were given to Helen Keller, Pasteur, Michelangelo, Mother Teresa, Leonardo da Vinci, Thomas Jefferson and Albert Einstein
(Brown H. J.)

Nobody owes you nothing, row your own boat

Whenever help is on hand, take it and don't be too proud about it either, because trust me, it will not come along very often. Do not expect any help in achieving your goals, because rarely is life fair and rarely will people offer you help along the way, however this way you will be pleasantly surprised when someone does offer assistance.

Expecting the world to treat you fairly because you are a good person is like expecting a bull not to attack you because you are a vegetarian
(Wholey)

You have to row your own boat in life because no one else will do it for you, because they are busy rowing their own boat – who can blame them? In the same way you have your own goals and ambitions, they will have their own so for every minute they spend helping you towards your goals, they are not working towards their own. So do not be surprised when even your best friend seems to be out for themselves and doesn't seem keen to help you, trust me I have been on the receiving end of this, it is not nice but again, be prepared for it. You cannot blame them really, they are looking out for their own interests, so you should be doing the same.

The men who try to do something and fail are infinitely better than those who try to do nothing and succeed
(Jones)

There is a chapter in this book on managing your own expectations and that is what you have to do here. Don't expect any help from anyone and you will not be disappointed. If you expect everyone to bend over backwards and drop everything to help you, you will be disappointed – and I included parents in this as well. Do not expect anything from anyone. Not only will it help manage your expectations but more importantly it will toughen you up mentally and teach you to fend for yourself.

That said however I am a big believer in that you should help others so do your bit when you can. A candle looses nothing when it lights another candle. I also believe what goes around comes around and the selfish people, who are out for themselves, rarely get any further in life than those who take the time to help others. It is your conscience and you have to live with it, so do what you think is right by others, but just do not expect anything back in return. You never know, the person you offer to help today, could be running a huge company tomorrow and they may just remember you and reward you for your efforts, but that should not be your motivating factor for helping people in the first place.

So keep on rowing that boat towards your goals and don't be too concerned about others providing any assistance. Don't make any plans involving others and you just keep doing your thing. That way when mum or dad offer to pay the deposit on that house, or in the in-laws offer to pay for the wedding or baby furniture, the world will seem just that bit of a nicer place.

In helping others, it helped me as much as it helped them. It's rewarding (Garcia)

There are two kinds of people, those who do the work and those who take the credit. Try to be in the first group, there is less competition there (Gandhi)

Be flexible to work – say Yes

What sort of day are you going to have tomorrow? Do you know already? Do you have any control of what type of day you will have tomorrow? Will it be successful, happy, stressful, jolly, depressing, good or bad?

Do you think you have any control over the day or does it depend literally on what side of the bed you get out of? Does YOUR day tomorrow depend on everyone else and how they may or may not affect you? Does YOUR day depend on the journey to work, if someone offers you a seat on the tube, if there is traffic on the way to the office, or is YOUR day determined by your colleagues in the office? What your boss says to you or if you get your lunch on time?
Or is it a combination of all these factors that will determine if you go home with a smiley face or a grumpy face? If you get into the office feeling good, then someone makes a negative remark, is that it for you, might you as well go home because you have allowed that one remark to ruin YOUR day? Which one of these factors is responsible for how your day will go?

It is none of the above.

Last time I checked, I am in control and I am responsible for my emotions, no one else. What determines the success of my day, is me. The success of your day is determined by YOU. I will not allow anyone else or any circumstance to belittle my own soul, by allowing it to mess my day up. Not one bit. I chart my success and I chart my course, yes there will be obstacles and distractions on the way, but the secret is this – don't let them affect you. And certainly don't let them affect your performance.

A pessimist sees the difficulty in every opportunity, an optimist sees the opportunity in every difficulty

(Churchill, 1874 - 1965)

Tomorrow morning when you wake up tell yourself you are going to have a good day and smile. Ok, don't overdo it and stare in the mirror saying 'I am a tiger' but inject some positive thoughts into your mind and tell yourself you are going to have a good day, then see what happens.

If you are the sort of person who allows the world to affect them every day, the rude chap on the tube train, the fact it is raining, the cat has made a mess on the kitchen floor, the delivery from that website is late, the coffee machine has run out, or the vending machine swallowed your money, whatever it may be, ask yourself am I so weak minded and easily detracted to allow these things to ruin my day?

Be strong, ignore these issues and don't sweat the small stuff. Rise above these minor distractions and remind yourself that you are a person on a mission to achieve your goals and push on working towards them. The best piece of advice I can offer is don't be precious about small issues. If you focus on the small stuff and place importance on the small things in life, you will think small and spend far too much effort on tiny elements of the bigger picture. You will still be moving towards your goals, but at a fraction of the speed you could be moving at, if you focused on the bigger picture.

Happiness is an attitude of mind, born of the simple determination to be happy under all circumstances

(Walters)

Don't listen to others, chart your own course

So many people fail at the first hurdle when trying something new because they listen to others. You will be amazed to learn that there is an expert, on every subject in the world, stood in your local pub right now. They are there telling anyone who will listen that they know best and you should 'not even bother' with your new idea. It drives me mad to think what these people get out of trying to destroy other peoples, ideas, dreams, beliefs and ambitions. Don't listen to them. Do not listen to them.

Nothing great was ever achieved without enthusiasm
(Emerson, 1803 - 1882)

Read some biographies of successful people you aspire to and they will tell you how often they were met with adversity. Nobody wanted James Dyson's idea for a bag-less vacuum so after years of trying to persuade the big companies of his idea, he went and made it himself. He is now Sir James Dyson and is estimated to be worth around £1billion.
Guess how many publishers turned down the Harry Potter series of books? It is reported that 12 publishers turned the book down. It was a year later when JK Rowling finally found one and they offered her an advance of £1,500. JK Rowling is estimated to be worth £1billion and has been awarded an OBE. How do you think Ms Rowling felt after the first 3 no's? How about after 6 no's in a row? What about once they got to 10 no's – surely people must have been saying to her at that point, "come on Jo, 10 no's, that must tell you something". But she clearly didn't listen and kept on trying and that is just often the difference between success and failure, the people who make it in life and those that do not.
You must not think that people who are now 'famous' or 'celebrities' have anything that you do not. They are no different from me and you and just because they have succeed with their idea or business, it does not mean they

must have been created different in some way and are godly beings with the divine right of success.

This is often the most basic difference between the successful people in life and the people who do not succeed. It is not always the case that their idea or invention is far superior to anything else, it's just that they stuck to their idea, didn't take no for an answer, persevered, kept on trying and ultimately succeed.

It is quiet normal to feel rather down trodden and question your work or ideas from time to time and there will be set-backs, but be prepared for them and manage your expectations. As I write this book now, I hope it will fly off the shelves and be a global best seller, however I am perfectly prepared and mentality primed if I only sell 5 copies – all to my mum!

It is exactly when we doubt our ideas , that it is just the time to focus even more on them, think about how you can make your idea better and also take onboard any feedback you have been given. But don't give up, keep going and don't listen to the doom-mongers.

Kites rise highest against the wind, not with it
(Churchill, 1874 - 1965)

Obstacles are those frightful things you see when you take your eyes off your goal
(Ford, 1863 - 1947)

Avoid the crowd. Do your own thinking independently. Be the chess player, not the chess piece
(Charell)

Enjoy work

Like it or not, work is something we all have to do. That's why I feel sorry for people who complain about work or their job. It is such a large factor in our lives and consumes many of our daily hours, so finding a job you enjoy or have a passion for, should take presidency over doing a job purely for the money.

Find a job you love and you never have to work another day in your life (Confucius)

That said whilst there are many jobs we may like to do, the reality is that we have to take jobs which pay sufficiently to ensure we can live the lifestyle we would like. For example as much as I would have like to become a full time ski instructor, unfortunately here in the UK I simply would not be able to earn enough money to do so.

Therefore although we may not be able to do the job we love, it is vital to ensure you enjoy the job you do. You probably don't need me to explain why it is important to enjoy work, suffice to say that countless studies show that people who are happy at work are more productive, communicate more with staff, and have better mental health and better personal lives as well. The opposite is true for those who do not enjoy work. Therefore doing a job you enjoy or feel challenged by, is a good thing and despite what the salary may be, you should where possible go with something you enjoy.

What I also want to mention is peoples approach to work which I feel especially amongst youth in the UK today is awful. I am repulsed by images of people signing on the dole and complaining of foreign workers taking their jobs. I saw a documentary a few months ago in which local young men were signing on and complaining of foreign workers taking their jobs. The journalist said there are plenty of jobs here in your town picking strawberries in the fields. The man said he didn't want to do that job and local farmers were forced to bring in foreign workers. So what do they expect? The perfect job right on their doorstep? They were not prepared to consider taking a job and working their way up the ladder.

We now have a society of people who understand the word 'Want' but are far less familiar with the word 'Work'. People are very keen to get the things they 'want' such as phones, i-pods, laptops, cars and designer clothes, but somewhere we seem to have lost the connection and association of these things with work. You have to work for the things we want, earn them and achieve a sense of pride and self admiration for the effort you put in to obtaining them. It is the sense of pride that helps teach people the value of items. The same item which you have worked hard for months to buy is much more valuable than the one which was given to you.

Therefore you should seek to enjoy work, take pride in what you do and reap the benefits of your hard work. Don't think of work as something you have to do, think of it as something you want to do and connect work with the things you desire. It is not easy and it will not happen by accident. You will be very lucky to leave school or University and walk into the perfect job at the right level. It can take time, and you will not instinctively know what the right career path is for you. But keep with it, don't be afraid to take side-ways steps, or even step back if it gets you on the right track.

The idle man does not know what it is to enjoy rest
(Einstein, 1879 - 1955)

The only place where success comes before work is the dictionary
(Kendall)

Don't be embarrassed to aspire to others

I think it is very important to have someone who inspires you, someone you admire, look up to or someone who you aspire to be. There is no shame in doing this aged 18 or 80.

I am proud to say I have been an admirer of Richard Branson, Alan Sugar, Warren Buffet, Lewis Hamilton, Jonny Wilkinson and Michael Thomas. I consider all of them to have enviable qualities, qualities that I too wish to have and feel would make me more successful. What's wrong with that?

What I don't like are people who belittle the achievements of others. These people are often the energy vampires and doom-pedlars of life who don't have a good word to say about anyone else. Typically they are simply jealous of other people's success and are envious.

It is ok to be envious of your neighbour, friend or colleague from time to time, because you can channel that energy as a force for good. If your colleague is performing better than you at work, take that as the shot in the arm you need, take that as motivation to start performing better. If your neighbours have a new conservatory, then use this to inspire you, take some energy and work harder so you can have the same thing if that is what you want.

I feel other peoples success is something to be studied and analysed because in there may lie some help and guidance to help you succeed and achieve your goals. I have already mentioned in this book about not being proud and taking help when it's offered. If there is anything you can learn or wisdom you can gain by studying others, do it.

I mentioned previously about James Dyson and his struggle to get his bag-less vacuum ideas accepted by the major manufactures at the time. He struggled to get them to accept the idea as commercially viable. So instead he set about making them himself. How do you think he felt at the time? Every major manufacturer has told him the idea will not work. What must he have thought when he started ploughing his own money and finances into his new idea? For example if a doctor gives you their expert opinion, you tend to listen to it. Likewise if the heads of an industry all tell you 'you are wrong' you do tend to listen to them also.

The point is he didn't because he believed in his idea.

It's reading about people like this and how they approached an obstacle and how they went about hammering and forging their own success, which can give you countless ideas and thoughts about how you can apply the same mindset and skills to your own success. So don't be embarrassed to read about the success of others, it is encouraging and inspiring and allow yourself to be immersed in it.

Be mindful of what you read and keep your own council about how to judge their writings. Try to avoid the rags to riches stories and preaching's of the super wealthy. There is an American billionaire, whose books I have read and they were just ridiculous preaching's and nothing note worthy about business or success. Read what appeals to you and take the bits that work for you.

So aspire to others yes, but just be mindful of who inspires you.

The man of genius inspires us with a boundless confidence in our own powers
(Emerson, 1803 - 1882)

I didn't aspire to just be a good sport, 'Champion' was good enough for me
(Perry)

Your SWOT analysis & appraisals

Have you recently undertaken a personal SWOT analysis on yourself? Do you not have a clue what I am talking about?

SWOT stands for **S**trengths, **W**eaknesses, **O**pportunities & **T**hreats and it is a form of analysis we use in business to assess a firm or a plan or strategy. But it works just as well when we do this for ourselves. Below is an example of how this can look:

Strengths	Weaknesses
Degree Education	Poor communication skills
Good work relations	Poor personal finances
Good contacts within firm	

Opportunities	Threats
Company promotion prospects	Competition at work from rivals
New qualifications & training	Increasing living & travel costs

The SWOT analysis can cover all elements of your life, work, family, social, play and anything else you feel relevant. It is important you enter the true answers and not the answers you would like to see. It can give you an honest assessment of where you are which may surprise you for both good and bad reasons. You may also want to consider the opinions of others when constructing your SWOT analysis.

Either way, you want the truth so you can then make informed decisions to make efforts in the areas that you feel need to be developed and help you exploit your strengths.

Doing this work can also be useful preparation before a job interview, it can help you judge how best to answer the various questions and give an accurate assessment of your current capabilities. This is also applicable to your current job and can be of real value during your appraisal.

Many people don't like having appraisals / performance reviews but I love them. I consider it my chance to ensure the boss knows about all the great things I am doing and ensure I give him/her no place to hide in recognising and rewarding my efforts through promotion and pay rises.
I cannot understand people who don't like them nor look forward to them, I can only think they are probably underperforming and know something is going to get said to them or they are concerned the boss may open a can of worms which they preferred was left alone.
You should go in fully prepared, armed to the teeth with ammunition of your achievements and why you deserve the recognition for what you do. Keep statistics, sales figures or whatever is relevant to your role and produce them with a touch of gloss and leave the boss with no place to hide.

As part of your preparation do a SWOT analysis and you can pre-empt potential issues the boss may raise. As such you can be prepared and armed with responses. For example if they say your communication needs improving, you can agree and tell how you have not only recognised the issue but also taken measures by booking yourself on a communication workshop. Therefore it is no longer an issue and you can move onto the subject of pay rises!

Job security is gone. The driving force of a career must come from the individual
(Bahrami)

It's just a job. Grass grows, birds fly, waves pound the sand. I beat people up.
(Ali)

Be like Water

This is about as philosophical as I am going to get, but the analogy of being like water is something that really resonates with me, so please bear with me on this chapter.

Water can fit into any shape of vessel, modify and adapt itself to fit. It can also easily be poured out of the vessel and into another.

Water can easily pass through any gaps and provides no resistance to get where it is going. It may pass through smaller gaps slower, but it doesn't stop and still gets there. Watch a river flow and you will see the water go around objects, over them, under them, through them, it will get to wherever it needs to go regardless of the route it needs to take.
Watch the journey it takes and you will see as it travels over rocks, waterfalls and even through the ground it comes out pure on the other side

Water cannot be compressed, it retains its mass regardless of the pressure put upon it and successfully resists any attempts to distort it due to the stress applied. Although it can change to any shape, it cannot be forced to reduce its mass.
No matter what pressure is applied it retains its mass but remains entirely flexible.

Water is clear and transparent, there is nothing hidden, you can see exactly what is in it and it is usually pure.
Water can travel thousands of miles in a river, through rapids and smoothes, over waterfalls and rocks. It keeps going, it never stops and always finds a way around obstacles.

Lastly it makes this journey time and time again as part of the water cycle. It falls as rain in the mountains and makes the journey of thousands of miles, only to do it all over again.

Hopefully from reading this you have gathered the point I am making ant will see how this analogy ties in with the chapters in this book.

Try and be like water in every situation of life, flexible and adaptable, resilient to pressure and relentless. Clear pure and transparent but tireless and aggressive.

It is astonishing what force, purity and wisdom it requires for a human being to keep clear of falsehoods
(Fuller, 1810 - 1850)

When we long for life without difficulties, remind us that oaks grow strong in contrary winds and diamonds are made under great pressure
(Marshall, 1902 - 1949)

In the confrontation between the stream and the rock, the steam always wins. Not through strength, but through persistence
(Unknown)

A little more persistence, a little more effort and what seemed hopeless failure may turn to glorious success
(Hubbard, 1856 - 1915)

Emotional Intelligence

This is one of my favourite subjects in business and life and its one some people just don't get. They don't understand their own impact on a situation and struggle to dispassionately and objectively view situations.

It's one of the main reasons why people hit a glass ceiling in their career because they develop a reputation for being difficult or get ahead of themselves. It can also explain why some people are good in some areas and poor in others.

For example a good manager needs to get the best out of his/her staff. However if your managing a team of 20 people, that's twenty different personalities, twenty different attitudes, egos and ambitions.
Therefore the manager cannot take a one-size fits all approach to managing all these different characters. They also have to understand how they themselves affect the dynamics of the team and the feelings of the individuals. They need to therefore be mindful of their own emotions, actions and feelings and manage them accordingly as they go about their work. As such they need to have the skills to speak, act and deal with different people differently to get the best out of them and ensure the manager achieves their desired outcomes. It can be tricky, demanding and requires a lot of patience on your part however having full control of your emotions is an excellent skill to have.

There is much debate over the exact definition of emotional intelligence, however I like to think of it in simple terms. It is controlling your emotions and affecting the emotions of others for a mutually agreeable outcome.
So if you're reading this and you are the sort of person who flies off the handle easily, thinks they are right all the time, is reading this very sentence and thinking what rubbish, then this chapter has been written for you.

Get over yourself, and do it now.

Forget about the journey and focus on the destination. If you have a job to get done and require others to help you do it then engage with them, manipulate them and praise them to help get what you need to get done. It's as simple as that. My suggestion is leave your ego at the door on the way into work and collect on the way out. Focus on getting the task done and treating staff in the exact way which ensures you get the maximum outcome.

Find out their motives. Some people like to be challenged and enjoy competition, others need constant praise, some people need reassurance and guidance from you, and some people have no initiative but can do things brilliantly once shown what to do. Either way it doesn't matter, after all you are focused on your goals, getting where you want to go, why does it matter how you get there? As long as the job gets done, does it really matter if it's not done in the exact way you would prefer? Don't be precious about little things.

Once the task is completed on time, ahead of time, below budget, then the praise will be there for you, what a great team leader you are and you will receive the rewards. Trust me it is worth it, so get emotionally intelligent now!

Another way of looking at this from the emotional point of view is to ask yourself, who is in charge of your emotions? There is a chap I worked with who had an inflated opinion of himself to start with, but almost every day as part of the usual office banter, he would get really wound up, annoyed, angry and embarrassed just by others saying a few jokes. He thought of himself as someone who was in control, cool and composed, but the slightest joke about him and he would flip. I asked him one day, who is in charge of your emotions? Before he could answer I told him I was. I said, I control your emotions and I choose if you have a good or bad day. He looked confused. I explained that if I planned to wind him up one morning, I could, and furthermore I knew how he would react. He would blow a fuse, become all frustrated and it would ruin his morning. I could play him like a fiddle and get any tune I liked.

I explained to him that he needed to take control of his emotions and remain in control regardless of what external influences tried to take over. He could decide and choose how he responded to anything that was said to him, he simply needed to take control over his emotions, he needed to rule them and not be ruled by them. You should learn to do the same.

The degree of one's emotions varies inversely with the ones knowledge of the facts
(Russell, 1872 - 1970)

The sign of intelligent people is their ability to control their emotions by the application of reason
(Mannes, 1904 - 1990)

Just as your car runs more smoothly and requires less energy to go faster and further when the wheels are in perfect alignment – you perform better when your thoughts, feelings, emotions, goals and values are in balance
(Tracy)

See the bigger picture - think outside yourself

People wrapped in them self make small packages and despite what you might think the world does not revolve around you. I am not suggesting you are so small minded to think this, however unfortunately there are people out there who think this way and as such unknowingly they massively restrict their potential. For those with natural emotional intelligence, this will be something they instinctively understand, however there are others out there that just don't get it.

I went into a convenience store the other day and as I was leaving the store when the women in front decided to stop, answer her mobile phone and have a conversation in the door way preventing others from entering and me from leaving. This is a pet hate of mine, but on a serious note how can you be so self absorbed to not realise that there are other people around you? The phone rings and you lose all sense of your surroundings? What if a piano was being lifted to a high rise flat when suddenly the cables snapped – but at the same time your phone rings, my guess is these people would answer the phone first. I sometimes wonder how these people are able to successfully cross the road. Have you ever had a driver behind you driving very close to the back of your car, they are desperate to get where they are going despite putting at risk their live and yours in the process to just get an extra 6 feet further up the road? Yes we all can be in a hurry sometimes but often these people rarely step back and see the bigger picture, they are too selfish with their own agenda.

Now I make a couple of small points here but you can imagine this on a larger scale. There are people in this world who do consider themselves very important or are self absorbed and they appear, dress, speak and act in a manner fitting their own self importance. Two things – don't buy any of it and don't let any of it put you off. They may very well have some good qualities but don't for one second think they are any better than you. Furthermore don't be intimidated by any of the show, all too often it is the most arrogant and cocksure people who have the least intelligence. They get along by intimidating others and appearing knowledgeable – they are not.

Thinking outside yourself is about understanding you and your place in your world. You are not the world but a player within your world, which also contains a variety other components such as work, family and friends. You need to have awareness on a mental level, because how you act, think and feel effects the world you live in.

A great example of this is when someone at work wants a pay rise. Too often I have seen people go about this entirely the wrong way because they only see things from one point of view, theirs. They are absorbed in their own world and don't understand they are a player in their world.
Because of this they tend to ask for money without providing justification and without regard to the feasibility of a pay rise within the companies budgets. What about the bank bailouts in 2008? Many people argued that the banks should have been allowed to fail. But this is a ridiculous argument because if the banks were allowed to fail, who would small businesses go to for banking and lending facilities if there are no banks? The majority of people in the UK work for small businesses, so the banks would have failed and so would thousands of small businesses. It is just this sort of short sighted thinking without real consideration. Many trade unions in the 70's had the view of protecting workers, but it became ridiculous and selfish greed took over which is unsustainable and shorted sighted. See the bigger picture and think about outside factors which affect you, because they will, as your life is not lived inside a vacuum.

A person without a sense of humour is like a wagon without springs, jolted by every pebble in the road.
(Beecher)

Say YES and be adaptable

Nothing frustrates me more than long term unemployed people who say there is no work out there. Yes there is. There are tons of jobs out there, but too many people turn work down because they either have too high opinion of themselves, demand a job which is within five minutes of their home, want top dollar pay, think the world owes them a living and if they don't get all that, turn the job down.

These people are not adaptable and cannot see past their own noses, they don't see a means to an ends and they are looking for the perfect job. The perfect job does not exist so they never find it. Sometimes in life you have to go with what you have, take what is in front of you and continue working towards your goals. For example when I first qualified as a financial adviser I took a job which was paying around 25% less than what I was earning previously. I took a pay cut as a means to an ends, I was qualified but needed experience advising and not many firms will take on someone who is not CAS (competent adviser status) so I worked for a firm that would offer me a role. I gained experience, worked hard and made good money for the company and myself, I then eventually set up my own firm. It was short term pain for long term gain and I am much better off as a result.

If you have an opportunity in front of you take it as you don't always know where it will lead. Don't restrict your potential opportunities by having a rigid mindset, as saying no and allowing things to pass you by will not help you achieve your goals. Be open to new opportunities and try not to see things as they are, but how they could be. Don't accept the stated norms regarding career paths or the text book routes, forget about all that and make your own path and chart your own route.

Therefore say YES more often than you say no and be flexible in your approach to achieving your goals. Make yourself attractive to potential employers and potential business contacts. Be out going and approachable and always leave a good impression. Think of yourself as an asset, you want to make yourself a valuable asset to your clients, employer, potential employers, colleagues, bosses and yourself. This way you will be valued and rewarded as people recognise a valuable asset and want to hang on to it.

Effective people are not problem-minded, they're opportunity minded.
They feed opportunities and starve problems

(Covey)

Always be investing

You should always aim to be investing, by that I mean putting something in, in expectation of getting a greater return.
To that extent you should aim to always be investing in everything you do and putting in maximum effort, safe in the knowledge that you may get a greater return.

This can take many forms. For example you can invest your time and effort into your job. Try really hard every day at work, give it your all, go beyond what is expected of you and really make a difference to your output. If you invest in that what can you expect as a return? A pay rise, promotion, responsibility, flexibility at work, favourable treatment, it could be any of these things. You may right now be thinking to yourself, that wouldn't happen in my job as I am not appreciated, they would never notice any extra effort so why bother? Really, well you have to shout about your own achievements, no one else will do it for you. So if you decide to invest time and effort into work, make sure that everyone knows about it!

My granddad is an amazing man and he worked for the council installing street lighting in Manchester for thirty years as a foreman. If you listen long enough he will tell you he installed every street light in Manchester! He once told me he had an interview with his boss which was an appraisal. These were fairly new things in the 60's and 70's. He was asked many questions, one of which was 'what is your value to the council in the role you do' and 'what do you think you are worth?' He laid it on thick, very thick. He said the council would collapse without him being there every day. That he was priceless and worth a million pounds per day to them for the work he does. He told them they couldn't pay him enough money and that they were lucky to have him!

So granddad went too far but do you see the point? You have to scream and shout about how good you are do not be put off by being shy or feel ashamed by blatant self promotion.

So what else can you invest in? You could decide to invest in yourself, start reading, attend a course, and put yourself forward for additional training. There is no greater investment, than investment in yourself – you tend to spend most of your life with your body and your mind so it is worth putting in the effort. This also includes fitness training, invest in your body and mind and get fit, you tend to use both body and brain most days so get them in top shape, you will look and feel better which will improve your confidence and ability to achieve your goals.

You can choose your type of investment but have a positive mind, invest for the long run and focus on the return. For example, you may choose to change career and retrain and that may mean you taking a pay cut. Is that an investment? Of course it is. If you are a shelf stacker and decide to retrain as a solicitor, that can be a great investment. It may take time, it may require you to take a personal loan to pay for your studies and you may earn less from work, but in the end you will be a qualified solicitor and they tend to earn more than shelf stackers. So the journey will have been worth it – assuming your aim was to earn more money and build a professional career.

You can also invest in your relationships, social and professional networks. You may want to create a strong professional reputation for yourself over the next 10 years across your profession. As such you need to invest in building relationships and contacts because rarely are great relationships a creation by accident. That means seeing the bigger picture and playing the long game. If you quote a potential client who eventually places their business elsewhere, you must part company not on good, but excellent terms. That way you have every chance of winning their business the following year, or maybe the year after that. The key is you don't have to do any more to win their business, you just need your competitor to make a mistake, and then they will come to you. Plus you will also attract referrals and recommendations. Investing in good relationships in business and in life is an excellent investment of your time. The saying is that most big deals happen on the golf course – and it can be very true.

The secret is to see the bigger picture. The people who cannot see past their own noses and snatch and grab at any bits of money they see rarely run successful businesses. They are the magpies, their heads easily turned by the first sight of anything shiny, before fleeing for the next shiny item. They don't stay the course, they are not in it for the long run, they don't invest, they do not put in the time, the effort, the graft and that's why they are always trying new things and failing. You should not do that, you should do the right thing and invest for the long term, firstly by investing in your most valuable asset - yourself.

Do not be proud

Ask for help when you need it, admit it when you get things wrong, change your approach when things don't go to plan, hold up your hands when you make mistakes and don't think your perfect because, I know and you know, you are not. What you can do however in these circumstances is study in great detail why things did not go to plan, why you were wrong, what mistakes you made and make sure you get it right next time.

There is no such thing as failure, only results, with some more successful than others
(Keller)

There is nothing wrong in failure, on the contrary it usually tells us exactly what we did wrong and therefore it should be studied as there is feedback in every failure. Critically you must adapt and change because there must be a reason why something went wrong or things didn't go to plan, it is not always down to circumstance – but it can be sometimes.

If you carry on doing the same old thing, the same old thing will keep happening to you. To change your future, renew your mind and do something new
(Unknown)

Because of this you must be prepared to make changes to your plans, your approach or your strategy, and certainly don't be too proud to do so.

They say real intelligence is knowing what you do not know and being aware of this, being comfortable in yourself and having the emotional intelligence to find a solution. Only a fool and the arrogant think they know everything and have the answer for anything. In fact it is often the case, that the arrogant throw themselves into things ignoring their short comings. There is a small degree of admiration to their approach however, often they simply demonstrate to the world their own stupidity. Not being proud relates very well to managing your own expectations. You know you are not a genius, but you are smart, you are bright and you do have good ideas. So make a start but manage your expectations that you may not crack it first time, become a worldwide sensation overnight or sell a million widgets in year one, but you may just make the first steps towards real success.

Don't forget there is a reason why Mark Zukerberg, Larry Berg or Chad Hurley are famous for their successes – because it's an exceptionally rare phenomenon. You tube was created in Feb 2005 and sold the following year for $1.65b making the people and early investors very rich, that is why it made the news so do not expect the same from your idea, manage your expectations and if that does happen, then all the better for you!

Knowing what you don't know is crucial to not being proud so ask for help and seek out the experts. Once you find them, do what you can to get as much information from them as possible. It would take you twenty lifetimes to become an expert at everything – so don't waste your time, recognise there are better qualified people in other areas than you. Don't resent them, applaud them and use them for your benefit. Trying to do everything yourself is a false economy. If you charge more than £500 per hour for your work as a professional, then in theory you should not spend any time doing any task which could be done by others for less. An accountant for example would not charge £500 per hour, so get them to do your tax return and you get busy working and earning £500 per hour.

A proud man is always looking down on people and of course, as long as you are looking down, you cannot see something that's above you
(Lewis, 1893 - 1963)

Graft

As mentioned previously, nothing of value is easy to acquire. Anything worth having is worth fighting for and as such hard work is what will get it for you.

Don't get me wrong either, I am like you, Monday morning 6am is never that pleasant and sometimes we all need a bit of a kick start, but the difference is, that despite the mild inconvenience, discomfort, pain or excruciating agony, the successful people carry on.

You might be surprised to know that this is usually the only difference between the successful people in life who achieve their goals and those that don't. Woody Allen says 80% of success is just showing up and I agree with him to a point. Get out and about, get your face seen, get in the office early, show some enthusiasm – don't drag yourself into work - have a spring in your step. On some days you may feel like a fraud but don't tell anyone, simply die on the inside and collapse when you get home from tiredness, its only pain and after all that's just an emotion controlled by the brain.

Pain is temporary. It may last a minute, or an hour, or a day, or a year, but eventually it will subside and something else will take its place. If I quit, however, it lasts forever

(Armstrong)

I know someone I worked with previously who was excellent at getting up and getting in the office early and working late. He was always enthusiastic towards the company and was keen to be seen working with senior managers. This is the point where Woody Allen forgot to mention that the other 20% is about talent and skill. As my ex-colleague had none, he still works for this company but has not moved on or has been promoted. Getting in the office early and staying late is great, but if you are simply browsing Facebook or the BBC Sport website then you're missing a trick.

Also brown nosing the bosses will only get you so far, a good manager should be interested in seeing results and revenue and not keen to hear how great you think they are.

Adversity reveals genius, prosperity conceals it
(Horace, 85BC - 5BC)

There are many simple terms in life which I like and live by such as - what can't speak can't lie, you only get what you pay for, and my favourite, you only get out what you put in.
If you only put in a half-arsed effort at work then only expect a half-arsed pay rise, promotion or prospects. Go to work every day and put in 100% effort then you will get this back in recognition, pay rise, promotion or headhunted by a firm that values your efforts. Either way don't lose sight of your goals so if you goal is to buy a place in Spain and your earnings are performance linked such as bonus or commission, then get grafting because what you do at work directly relates to achieving your goals. Because the moment you take your eye off your goals you start seeing objects that were not there previously and you start expending precious energy on non productive things.

The quote below sums up my approach to life well. Smooth seas never make a skilled sailor, neither does weak opposition make a strong football team. It is in adversity and difficulties that we really learn and develop our skills, it is when we have the battle scars to show and remind us of what we have overcome. What is hard to bare is always sweet to remember. So seek out challenges and throw yourself at them. Put yourself forward at work to take on a new task, put yourself on the front line because that is where the greatest people are created. Be one of them.

Smooth seas never made a skilled sailor
(Clay S. L., 2011)

Be open for business & communicate

Communication skills are vital in life and if there is one area I would encourage you to work on and seek training is communication skills. I genius who cannot explain his workings in a manner which makes people want to listen, may as well not have bothered in the first place. If Einstein was a shivering wreck, incapable of presenting his ideas, would the world have known about his workings? Probably yes, but he was exceptional, what about people on the fringe who struggle to get heard, sometimes you have to present well before people will even consider your ideas and grant you the audience you require.

At least that's my thinking and that's why the scientists and PHD's are rarely the ones running the country or large businesses. They are the 'boffins' and the 'geeks' we put in labs and libraries to produce the technical information we need to get on with our businesses. They are not the ones steering the ships or leading because, they cannot influence, inspire, lead and persuade effectively if they are no good at communicating their ideas. That is not meant in a derogatory way, it is simply to illustrate the different talents we all have and how best to use them. For example, if the human race was dependent on Alan Sugar performing chemical equations and physics, I would be deeply worried. But if the human race relied on someone capable of leading and organising people in the most effective way to combat a problem, Lord Sugar would be the man, and that's my point.

The reality of the world is that we like people who are well polished, can give a good presentation, speak well and look the part. Just look at the comparison between Tony Blair & Gordon Brown. Consider the job Winston Churchill did in leading us to victory in WW2. Could have Gordon Brown done the same job? I doubt it, but technically he had a lot of very good qualities and largely credited with leading the world by opting to bail out the banks. Would you be inspired to follow Gordon Brown to your certain death in battle? I am not saying I would do the same for Tony Blair or David Cameron but I hope you see my point.

Why is communication so important? If someone is to stand in front of you and deliver an important message, of the information you receive and interpret:

7% of the message will be based on the actual words and content
38% based on the way in which the message is said
55% based on non verbal communication.

So if I stand in front of you and give you an important message, 93% of the way I communicate with you, has nothing to do with the words I am using.

Too many people go through life frustrated as they do not feel valued. They feel they have a great deal to offer yet no one listens to them, their employer doesn't recognise their value, nobody seriously considers their ideas or suggestions and as such they lose the will to fight and become retrenched in their own frustration and bitterness. They blame the cruel world for not giving them a chance – the truth is they never gave themselves a chance.

In life you sometimes have to sharpen your elbows to get yourself on the platform and in front of the right people – but once you are there, it's your chance to perform and you have to do so, you may not get a second chance.

And the poor souls who feel dejected never gave themselves a chance because they didn't take the time to consider the fact that their poor communication is just as much to blame for their ideas and suggestions being overlooked. Being a genius in this world is sadly not enough, so learn how to deliver a good presentation, write an intriguing report or know how to internally publicise yourself. You need to grab people's attention.

Have confidence and some passion in your ideas, because that in itself breeds confidence from others in your abilities. Park the self doubt (because everyone has some) and be confident, chest out, take your moment on the stage and deliver your thoughts and ideas. Don't be afraid to use some artistic license in there either, do what it takes get their attention, and then knock them out with your ideas.

The trouble with the world is that the stupid are cocksure and the intelligent are full of doubt.
(Russell, 1872 - 1970)

Take their ammunition away from them

My mum actually told me about this many years ago at school when dealing with any conflict I had at school. I was lucky at high school, I got along with everyone and successfully mixed with all groups, I was on the football team and in with the 'cool' people but also good friends with the 'geeks' and all the other social groups which form at most schools. However from time to time there were the odd conflicts, no different to your schooling. One thing my mum would always say is 'kill people with kindness' and I feel that this is just as applicable for school kids as it is for adults in business. However I like to think of it slightly different, by which I put it, if you take someone's bullets away, they cannot shoot you.

So how do I apply this in day-to-day business? I once took the role as head of new business at a company which was historically very 'sales' resistant. My job was to inject a sales culture into the office, implement systems and processes to help drive new business sales. I knew from the outset that the staff would be very sceptical to me and my approach. They were experienced professional 'advisers' and didn't see themselves as 'sales people'. The reality is simple, the greatest photographer that has ever lived may open their own studio, but they will fail and be out of business fast if they cannot convince others to part with their cash for their photos. As such they must be able to sell themselves or their product or service, they cannot depend on talent and skill alone.

Anyone in business, has to be in sales.

So the team I inherited were sales resistant and reluctant to be involved with sales, which was deemed a dirty word.
So from day one I took their ammo away from them.
I knew (or at least had a very good idea) what their thoughts were and what their objections would be to me and my new role. I immediately set about holding a sales meeting and in

that meeting I stole all their ammo over the first few weeks. I told them that I knew what they were thinking. It worked because I was right. I had second guessed their initial perceptions of me, I had worked out what their stereotypical predetermined opinion of me and my ideas would be, and I highlighted all this in the first few meetings and met this issue head on.

I explained to them that I knew that they were expecting me to be a 'cheesy' sales guy and that I wanted to 'touch base' with them all. I explained that I don't use lots of management speak and that actually adding a sales element to what they already did would be of massive to benefit to them first and foremost.

What materialised over the coming weeks was a very harmonious working environment. I had demonstrated from the start that I knew, understood and appreciated their concerns. By addressing these issues head on, right from the start, I was able to not only empathise with them, but remove any potential future criticism from them as I had already second guessed their objections. This gave me instant credibility and respect in that they knew, I knew, their concerns.

You can apply this to any scenario, a difficult meeting, training, presentation, networking or conference. You can also use it very effectively in your personal life as well. If you take time to explain to people that you understand their objections, concerns, doubts, they know you are on their wavelength. So going back to my example as Sales Manager, at no point going forward could anyone turn to me and say you don't understand how we work – because I had already done this from day one. I had explained I knew their concerns, therefore they could not come back with the same concerns 6 months in the future as I had already addressed the issue.

Taking peoples ammo away from them is also a great way to avoid any criticism. I am ok at Golf, pretty good at football and awful at snooker. Therefore whenever I play snooker I always ensure I let everyone know I am rubbish at snooker. I inoculate against any potential criticism. Then when we are playing snooker nobody can turn to me and call me rubbish – because I have already told them that, they are not telling me anything I don't already know, and in the English language that is when criticism does not work.

If I am in a meeting and I don't know something, I will immediately let everyone know I have no experience in this area, that way I can receive no criticism for not knowing. The moment you start pretending you know more than you do, allowing others to think you understand or trying blag your way through a meeting – trust me you will be found out and your credibility damaged. So don't do it. Show you are comfortable in letting people know this is not an area of expertise for you, people will respect you for saying so and it demonstrates wisdom, because you know what you don't know.
Own the agenda of a meeting or discussion and get the information out there and tell people you know what you don't know. Showing people and explaining that you recognise what you don't know is a strong trait of intelligence so don't be ashamed about doing it. The shame of being found out will be so much worse.

Always forgive your enemies, nothing annoys them so much
(Wilde, 1854-1900)

When I was a kid I used to pray every night for a new bicycle. Then I realised that the Lord doesn't work that way so I stole one and asked him to forgive me
(Philips)

Destroy enemies by making them friends

Enemies does sound rather strong, however the reality is that there are people in our lives who we may not like, not get along with or people who have taken a dislike to you for whatever reason. The easiest thing is to avoid these people outright but often we have to work with these people, live next door to them, or in some cases are married to them! There is a chap I work with who as far as I can see, does not get along with anyone, I don't know why but he seems to take a dislike to many people for all manner of reasons. This can be career debilitating but he cannot see past the initial emotion of dislike and as such chooses to restrict his progression.

There will be people who you have fallen out with, had disagreements with or are seen as a threat to your career objectives. Either way along the journey of life there will be these people in all different forms and what you need to do is deal with them quickly.

Hatred only destroys the people who hate. The easiest way to get rid of enemies as quickly as possible, in the world of business and in our lives is to turn them into friends.

Hatred is the toxic waste in the river of life
(Unknown)

The most simple and effective way to get rid of our enemies is to make friends of them. I don't for one minute buy the 'keep friends close and enemies even closer' saying, don't have enemies in the first place would be my saying. That's surely is a much smarter way to manage people. Why do you want enemies and why would you want to keep them close?

Sometimes you have to face facts and it can often be the case that in life we have to work and live with people that we may not be fully compatible with. But that doesn't mean you

102

cannot work or live alongside them. It won't necessarily be bliss and harmony but you can make it work, and work is the crucial word. Because rarely do great relationships happen out of the blue or on a chance meeting, good relationships do not happen by accident but they take time, hard work, effort and commitment.

So think about the people at work tomorrow and think what can you do to turn them from enemies (or at least people you dislike) to people you do like. Put the effort in and take the initiative yourself. Be the one who goes the distance to build bridges and develop the relationship, because you should always be investing and you never know where things may lead. That person who you never got along with all of a sudden can become someone you in fact have lots in common with and become close co-workers. They may be the person that puts you forward for a promotion, or gives you a great referral to a new client.

The point is you don't know and you will never know unless you make the effort. Otherwise you are choosing to close yourself off to the world and others and that could be holding back your career or your progress towards achieving your goals.

Whenever you are in conflict with someone, there is one factor that can make the difference between damaging your relationship and deepening it. That factor is attitude.
(James, 1842 - 1920)

True friends stab you in the front
(Wilde, 1854-1900)

Achieve Your Goals

This final section of the book is the shortest part, and deliberately so, because goal setting and motivation is an entire book all on its own and I do not want to start covering too wide a range of topics. My focus is on helping people get on in life and work and managing their money. However achieving your goals is a personal thing to you, because the previous sections on managing money and managing yourself can be applied to anyone in any circumstance, goals and your goals, are personal to you.

However what I hope to do in this section is give you an introduction to goal setting and give you some structure as to how to set them and the process through which you can take. Because it was not that long ago that I did not do any goal setting nor have any awareness of the benefits.

Put simply having goals is vital to being successful in life because rarely does success just land on your lap, you need direction, you need a target, you need something to shoot for. Many people don't like the thought of this but regardless whether they like it or not, the fact is it gives everyone some direction. Some people object as they don't want to be 'defined' or feel like they are being told what to do. These uncontrolled emotions are just ordinary insecurities.

The key differentiator which I feel is important to stress however is how we all define success? Is success running a large business, climbing the corporate ladder, lecturing the next crop of graduates, achieving the pinnacle and accolades of your profession, raising a family or being a good parent or all of the above? These are all versions of success which can all have different meanings for different people. What is your definition of success? Ask yourself that question and take as long as you need to answer.

Goal setting

Goal setting is a very important part of achieving your goals, because rather obviously, it is the very setting of them which determines your direction.

If you want to live a happy life, tie it to a goal, not to people or things (Einstein, 1879 - 1955)

Furthermore it is not an event, but an ever evolving process which should be reviewed regularly.

A goal or objective is a desired result a person plans and commits to achieve, a personal desired end-point in some sort of assumed development. Many people endeavour to reach goals within a finite time by setting deadlines.

The most common time for many people to do goal setting is usually between Christmas and New Year. This often coincides with setting New Year resolutions and seems an appropriate time as one year ends and a new one begins. I would agree with this and suggest this can be a good time to do some goal setting. However you should try and take time out every few months to review your goals and check to see if you are on track, perhaps every quarter, or every six months, but it does depend on the timescales of the goals you have set.
Either way you want to ensure that what you are doing is moving you towards your goals because it can be easy for you to get side tracked, distracted and be working very hard, but not on the correct route to your goals.

So what is a goal? The goal is the destination, it is the main outcome of your efforts. It should be something appealing and attractive and something that should drive you to work toward it. Now you can have short term goals as well as long term goals, but I prefer to break them down into aims and objectives which are covered in the next chapter.

To understand more about goals it can help to ask yourself what current goals have you set yourself, have you done any previous goal setting? Get rich and famous is not a goal, nor is buying a mansion in Spain and marrying a supermodel, however all very appealing things I will agree.

Although these items are appealing and motivating, simply wanting to buy a villa in Spain will not necessarily mean you will get one, and that is the point of goal setting. You could work all your life in a low paid job wanting to buy the villa, but you will not get it from simply wanting alone. My dad used to say there are workers and wanters. Wanters spend all day thinking about what they want and what they would do with it when they get it. Workers are out there earning the money to buy the damn thing in the first place, and that's the difference. The workers eventually get there and the wanters never do. It is much easier to be wanter than a worker by the way.

You need to set a goal which will deliver the outcome, by which, you can then go and purchase your villa – just wanting something really badly is not enough unfortunately.
Before we move on however I do believe it is important to visualise the items you do want, Aston Martin, Ferrari, 10 bedroom villas, because these things do provide motivation and it doesn't hurt to take a few minutes out to think about what type of leather interior you would like for your Aston Martin DBS, but don't get carried away.

So the goal needs to be the outcome, of the plan, which gets you the villa. Or in other words, work backwards from your desires to create the goal and then the plan. In the same way you would plan a road trip, the goal setting is plotting your course towards the goal, but you need to know the destination first.

So it is certainly not my place to tell you what your goal should be. I have listed examples of what some people may chose to have as their goal but they are just examples and please do not let them prejudice your decision.

Think about what you want most and then think about how you would want to achieve it. For example financial freedom may be a common goal for a lot of us but there are a number of routes to get there. Start your own business, work hard in your current job, start a second business from home, take a second job, start developing property? You need to choose the route that suits you and go out there and achieve your goal!

Nobody succeeds beyond his or her wildest expectations unless he or she begins with some wild expectations

(Charell)

Aims

Now you know what the goal is, because you have taken time to consider it and have put a lot of thought into it. Therefore I am sure your goal is one which I would suggest is perfectly achievable for someone who is prepared to work for it.

A goal without a plan is just a wish

(Elder)

The next step now then is to create some aims, these are high level targets which will get us to our goal. Aims could act as milestones which chart our path towards the goal and give us benchmarks to understand and measure our progress. Aims should be seen as desirable things we want to achieve which not only drive us towards the goal, but also inspire us and create a desire within us to want to achieve the goal.

One aim may be to achieve £100,000 turnover in the first year of starting a new business. Another aim may be to achieve £500,000 turnover in year 3 and another aim can be to achieve turnover of £1,000,000 by year 5. Based on this we now have 3 high level aims, all of which interlink nicely and will help us to achieve the goal which may be for a new firm to generate turnover of £1,000,000 in five years.

It is important to remember that achieving the goal is the most important part, aims are just the benchmarks along the way. So in the above example, if you fall short and turnover is less than £100k in the first year, that does not necessarily mean you will not achieve your goal over the remaining four years. However you may need to re-evaluate the aims – but not always in every case. In this example there could be a perfect reason why turnover is less than expected in year one, however due to pent-up demand in the market, you could easily make up the sales in the following years and still be on track to achieve your goal.

Crucially the aims should be viewed as desirable outcomes, who wouldn't want £100,000 turnover in year one, so they do need to be mini motivators and not just measures.

I mentioned earlier the reason why I feel you should also incorporate aims and objectives into your goal setting.
Setting the goal but not a detailed plan on how to get there is pointless in every sense of the word.
So we have covered aims, now for objectives…..

If you do not know where you are going, how can you expect to get there?
(Walsh)

Objectives

We have our goal and we have some high level aims, we now need to think about objectives. Objectives are more specific targets that will help to achieve the aim which in turn moves us closer to the goal.

Considering the previous example from the last chapter, the new start up firm has a goal of achieving £1,000,000 turnover in 5 years with the aim of achieving £100,000 turnover in year one. Therefore if we look at year one turnover how will they achieve this?

They should set some objectives for year one which could be any of the following:
- Launch website within first month for online trade
- Run monthly promotions on specific products
- Create 3 affinity relationships
- Join local business networking club
- Recognition from trade industry bodies
- Recruit 2 European distributors

It all depends on the business and these are just examples but hopefully you see the point.

I feel I must also highlight at this point, that this method works just the same with personal goals as well.

Objectives are not quite day-to-day measures but more weekly or monthly benchmarks. They are more practically focused in terms of, what you actually will do, rather than high level. Crucially they are more time focused than aims or the goal and they should be aligned closely with a time scale. This is because if the objectives are not completed on time, they slip. If the objectives start slipping, then so do the aims and so on and so on….before you know it you are well behind schedule and having to re-evaluate everything all over again.

110

It is easy to get carried away with setting objectives and the secret is not to set too many, otherwise you end up chasing your tail and going round in circles. You also start looking at some objectives which you have achieved, and others you have not, and start working on percentages. All objectives are compulsory and must be completed.

It must be borne in mind that the tragedy of life does not lie in not reaching your goal. The tragedy of life lies in having no goal to reach
(Mays, 1895 - 1984)

Make your Goals, Aims & Objectives S-M-A-R-T

This book is not a sales manual however you may have come across SMART objectives. If you have ever attended a course or any form of training at work, then you may be familiar with the term.

SMART stands for:
Specific, **M**easurable, **A**chievable, **R**ealistic, **T**ime-based

When setting your goals, aims and objectives, cross check what you plan to do with the SMART check list and give your plans a reality check. This way you will ensure you are not aiming too high and that the objectives will get you towards the aim and the goal.

There is nothing more useless than creating objectives that don't help you achieve the goal. Now although this seems obvious time and again, I have been in class teaching students who have not created objectives which directly help them achieve the goal. It is not as straight forward as you think and I would encourage you to seriously think long and hard about setting objectives. I say this because if you get it wrong at the start and head along the wrong path, you can end up far away from where you wanted to be, much like a rocket being fired, fractional changes in trajectory can make a big difference to where it lands.

There is a saying, what you find depends largely on what you are looking for. That is why it is so important to ensure you set the right objectives which take you along the right path towards your goal.

Any person who selects a goal in life which can be easily achieved, has already defined their own limitations
(Robert)

Specific

Make sure you know what you are aiming for and be sure to drill down into the detail. Make sure you know what you need to do and give yourself a clear objective. If you are aiming for a monetary figure, then list it pounds, shilling and pence.

Measurable

This will help you to know when you have achieved it, or if not, how far short you were. You need to have a measure so you know what is close and when you have done it. For example, if your objective is to ensure every customer you have is happy when they leave your store......how do you know if you achieved the objective? Don't waste your time thinking about how you can measure every customer's level of 'happiness' just change the damn objective because it's a stupid one! Make it something you can easily measure and record.

Achievable

The target must be attainable. Striving for improvement is encouraging, striving for perfection is demoralising. You must therefore know it can be done based on others achievements or your own sound judgment. That said, the objective must be challenging, it must be motivating, it must require significant effort to achieve, because that's the whole point. If you set an objective to arriving at work on time every day, then ask yourself, how do I improve on that next time?

Realistic

Wanting to become a Premier League professional footballer is a great goal to have. However, if you are overweight and aged 45, give it up mate, because it just is never going to happen. Setting up a new social networking website to rival Facebook is an unrealistic aim. But don't forget these are just aims and objectives, they are not limits or restrictions. Aim to build a good website and focus your objectives on the quality of your work, not on what you 'hope' to achieve. Make them realistic and if you are an overnight success then good for you. Just focus on putting in 100% effort and the cream will always rise to the top.

Time based
All goals, aims and objectives should be set to a time line or deadline or you should aim to achieve them over a specific time frame. For your goals, the time line could be measured over years, aims over months and objectives over weeks, but it all depends on what goals you have set yourself and how you intend on achieving them.

Objective setting aside, use the SMART system in everything you do where appropriate. I feel it's a great sanity check for anything you want to do. It helps to manage your own expectations and the expectations of others as discussed in previous chapters.

I am currently playing golf as my main hobby and past time. It can be a very frustrating game and takes a lot of time and patience. Some days I play brilliantly and others I can barely hit the ball. I have purposefully set myself tough objectives for my golf game. But I always cross check them to ensure they are smart, it is not realistic for me to reach a specific level, then I will become de-motivated, uninterested and probably at some point quit the game altogether.

Personal Development

The final chapter of this book is on personal development. I want to leave you with my thoughts on why this should be your most important focus over the next 12 months if you are seriously committed to achieving your goals.

You are your greatest asset, not your possessions, cars or jewellery, it is you. Because without you your possessions are someone else's but more importantly where as possessions can come and go, you will always be inside your body and it is you that has to make use of your body and mind every day. It is your body and your mind that will get you where you want to go, possessions cannot. Do not think buying books and computers will make you intelligent, it is you and your mind that has to do the reading, and you have to do the studying. Do not think that buying a new car will attract the attention of the opposite sex, it is you that has to speak, charm and socialise. Anyone basing their success around possessions and objects will quickly be found out and it will not take others long to see through the thinly veiled layer of superficial materialism. People who attend social events and simply talk about their house or their car quickly run out of conversation and quickly bore others

You are your greatest asset and you therefore want to use your greatest asset for your benefit and to great effect.

You should constantly be investing in yourself, in you and in your ideas, dreams, motivators, ambitions, desires and goals. You want to fully arm yourself with the best possible weaponry money can buy. You want to be a walking weapon of mass attraction to others, be it employers, customers or the opposite sex.

Equip yourself with the tools you need to succeed at job interviews, perform well in your career, influence and manage others, become highly skilled and respected in your chosen field, a hit at every dinner party you attend, comfortable socialising and relaxing with friends, an excellent mother or father, achieve influence and respect amongst your peers and be an old round bloody nice person!

None of the above is easy nor is it acquired overnight, it requires constant ongoing investment in you. So how do you invest in yourself?

Attending courses and training, seek out successful peers and learn from them, ask lots of questions, put yourself forward and volunteer, network and socialise with people who can help you move up the ladder, make many friends, do not burn bridges, remember important information – names and faces, move in the right circles, to name just a few.

You should also pay particular importance to the soft skills. All too many people feel once they have a degree that is an instance access pass to any job and also gives them instant seniority amongst peers. Rarely is this the case. Often it is the people who can charm and influence, network and create alliances that get ahead in life (but they can also have a degree as well). These skills are so important in the modern world and I would urge you strongly to seek out training in these areas. There are local public speaking clubs which you can join, as public speaking is often a big fear for many people, it is something you should seek to overcome quickly.

Throughout all of this you should start to develop self awareness, which is recognising yourself and how you fit in, knowing your own flaws and weakness and recognising this yourself, instead of others recognising them for you. It means understanding that you don't operate your life in a vacuum.

I can tell you this now, if you constantly seek to invest in yourself, achieving your goals will become much easier, you will achieve them quicker and be capable of far exceeding them.

God helps those who help themselves
(Franklin, 1706 - 1790)

Who has confidence in himself, will gain confidence of others
(Lazarow)

Your chances of success in any undertaking can always be measured by your belief in yourself
(Collier, 1885 - 1950)

Getting ahead in a difficult profession requires avid faith in yourself. That is why some people with mediocre talent, but with great inner drive, go so much further than people with vastly superior talent
(Loren)

I am indeed a King because I know how to control myself
(Aretino)

The aim of life is self development. To realize ones nature perfectly – that is what each of us is here for
(Wilde, 1854-1900)

Formal education will make you a living, self education will make you a fortune
(Rohn)

I hope you have enjoyed reading this book and I hope it has given you some real ideas about how to go about achieving your goals. Get your finances in to shape over the coming months and that will give you the platform then to start launching your new ideas and plans for your life.

Think about the many soft skills from chapter two, start saying yes, be open and communicative and stop waiting for things like luck. You do not need luck, you have all the talent in the world to get where you want to go. You just need the energy and the drive and remember to stay motivated. By all means read other books on motivation. Zig Ziglar said 'motivation doesn't last, well neither does bathing, that's why it's recommended daily.

Good luck and I hope you achieve your goals.

S L Clay

Works Cited

Ali, M. (n.d.).
Aretino, P. (n.d.).
Armstrong, L. (n.d.).
Bahrami, H. (n.d.).
Bank of England. (2011, January 15). *BOE Website*. Retrieved from Bank of England: http://www.bankofengland.co.uk/index.htm
Beecher, H. W.
Bombell, S. (n.d.).
Branson, S. R. (n.d.).
Brown, H. G.
Brown, H. J. (n.d.).
Buffet, W. (n.d.).
Buscaglia, L. F. (1924 - 1998).
Charell, R.
Charell, R. (n.d.).
Churchill, S. W. (1874 - 1965).
Clay, C.
Clay, S. L. (2011).
Collier, R. (1885 - 1950).
Confucius.
Covey, S. R.
Derek, B. (n.d.).
Diana, P. o. (n.d.).
Eastwood, C. (n.d.).
Edison, T. (1847 - 1931).
Einstein, A. (1879 - 1955).
Elder, L. (n.d.).
Emerson, R. W. (1803 - 1882).
Ford, H. (1863 - 1947).
Franklin, B. (1706 - 1790).
Frick, J. W. (1923 - 2008).
Friedman, R. (n.d.).
Fuller, M. (1810 - 1850).
Gandhi, I. (n.d.).

Garcia, K. (n.d.).

Gide, A. (1869 - 1951).

Glickman, L. J. (n.d.).

Hawking, S. (n.d.).

Hoffer, E. (n.d.).

Hope, B. (n.d.).

Horace. (85BC - 5BC).

HSBC. (2011, January 15). Retrieved from HSBC UK:
http://www.hsbc.co.uk/1/2/personal/savings/online-bonus-saver

Hubbard, E. (1856 - 1915).

James, W. (1842 - 1920).

Jones, L.

Keller, J. (n.d.).

Kendall, D. (n.d.).

Kirkham. (2010).

Kiyosaki, R. T. (2002). *Rich Dad Poor Dad.* Time Warner.

Kleiser, G. (1868 - 1953).

Larson, E. (n.d.).

Lazarow, L. (n.d.).

Lewis, C. S. (1893 - 1963).

Loren, S. (n.d.).

Mackay, H. (n.d.).

Mannes, M. (1904 - 1990).

Mansfield, K. (1888 - 1923).

Marden, O. S. (1850 - 1924).

Marshall, P. (1902 - 1949).

Mason, J. (n.d.).

Mays, B. E. (1895 - 1984).

Nationwide Vechile Contracts. (2011, January 16). Retrieved
from http://www.nationwidevehiclecontracts.co.uk/Vauxhall-Insignia-leasing.htm

Office of National Statistics. (2011, February 09). Retrieved
from http://www.statistics.gov.uk/cci/nugget.asp?id=285

Orben, R. (n.d.).

Owens, J. (1913 - 1980).

Parker, D. (1893 - 1967).

Perry, F. (n.d.).
Philips, E. (n.d.).
Robert, C. (n.d.).
Rogers, W. (1879 - 1935).
Rohn, J. (n.d.).
Rudner, R. (n.d.).
Russell, B. (1872 - 1970).
Russell, B. (1872 - 1970).
Saint-Evremond, C. d. (1610 - 1703).
Stein, W. H. (n.d.).
Tesco Finance. (2011, January 16). *Loan Calculator*. Retrieved from http://www.tescofinance.com/personal/finance/finance/loans /calculateLoanRepayment.do
The AA. (2010, January 16th). *AA Car Buyers Guide*. Retrieved from The AA: http://www.theaa.com/cbg/goodadvice/commongoodadvice.j sp?menu1=1&menu2=3&fileName=depreciation
Tracy, B. (n.d.).
Unknown. (n.d.).
Vauxhall UK. (2011, January 16). Retrieved from http://www.vauxhall.co.uk/vehicles/vauxhall-range/cars.html
Walsh, B. S. (n.d.).
Walters, J. D. (n.d.).
What Car. (2011, January 16). *Car Depreciation Calculator*. Retrieved from http://www.whatcar.com/car-depreciation-calculator/results?makeId=2080&modelVersionId=4112&editi onId=4163
Wholey, D. (n.d.).
Wikipedia. (2011).
Wilde, O. (1854-1900).
Your Mortgage.co.uk. (2011, February 09). Retrieved from http://www.yourmortgage.co.uk/news/3626468

About the Author

Scott Clay was born in 1981 in Manchester and was raised in Didsbury, South Manchester. As a typical middle child, the middle of three brothers, he often sought attention through merit, skill or blatant showing off.

His parents divorced at an early age which caused the breakup of the family and the brothers, with Scott and his younger brother leaving Didsbury to live in emergency accommodation. It was during this time that Scott feels his strongest desires of ambition and success are rooted. It was the shock change in living standards and conditions and the effect this had on his mother, which he credits with providing his driving ambition today.

Scott moved back to Didsbury when his mother remarried and attended school before leaving for the University of Hertfordshire studying a degree in Engineering in year 2000. However he quickly found that Engineering was not his subject and moved back to Manchester to study Business the following year. He achieved a HND in Business with merit before moving to Manchester Metropolitan University to complete his Ba(Hons) in Business & International Business. During all his time at University Scott worked part time to earn money to support him through his studies. He worked for a UK Bank as a sales adviser weekday evenings and some overtime at weekends. It was whilst studying business and working for the bank Scott found his passion for finance and business and a real head for managing money. He gained a lucrative space on the BEST programme during his final year at university which was designed for high calibre graduates showing excellence in business & entrepreneurship.

Scott finished his final exam at University in June 2004 on a Friday and started his first job the following Monday working for a UK software vendor. Scott quickly excelled in his new business role achieving great success and accolades within the company developing a UK sales channel. It was a chance event in Spain which Scott was asked to attend which led to his promotion after just 12 months to European Sales Manager. Travelling extensively across Europe managing a large sales channel was a fantastic opportunity for someone at such a young age. He brought in record sales and growth figures for the territory during his time in the role. Scott was promoted the following year to a UK major accounts role following his success in Europe working with some of the UK's largest IT companies.

Scott moved back into the finance sector in 2006 and became qualified as a financial adviser. It was during this time that his property development business was taking off and he was busy renovating, selling, refurbishing and letting properties across Manchester. Scott still prides himself to this day of being able to fit and install kitchens, bathrooms and central heating systems!

Scott created his own firm Clay Mortgages Ltd which ultimately became Didsbury Financial Planning Ltd providing clients with financial advice, helping people buy their first home, helping people out of debt and creating a plan for someone's retirement are still the pleasures which Scott gets from his role today. Scott is also a qualified teacher, lecturing on subjects including Business, Management, Education, Communication and Purchasing at local Colleges. He also teaches people how to learn to Ski which is another passion of his and is a qualified Ski Instructor. He is a member for the IFS School of Finance, the Chartered Management Institute, Institute for Learning and British Association of Ski Instructors.

He is also useless at golf, but insistent he may still make it as a pro golfer one day!

Contact the Author

I would welcome the opportunity to hear from anyone who has purchased this book and would like to give me feedback. I am always looking for ways to improve so please email me below, connect with me on Linkedin and follow me on Twitter.

Network Selection is my publishing and Consultancy business.

Network Selection
scott@networkselection.co.uk
www.networkselection.co.uk

Linkedin.com
http://uk.linkedin.com/in/scottclay

Twitter.com
ScottClay_Dfp

Kind regards
S L Clay